PEACE IS
EVERY STEP

Thich Nhat Hanh

PEACE IS
EVERY STEP

*The Path of Mindfulness
in Everyday Life*

Edited by Arnold Kotler

BANTAM BOOKS

NEW YORK · TORONTO · LONDON
SYDNEY · AUCKLAND

CONTENTS

vi

Foreword

BY H. H. THE DALAI LAMA

Although attempting to bring about world peace through the internal transformation of individuals is difficult, it is the only way. Wherever I go, I express this, and I am encouraged that people from many different walks of life receive it well. Peace must first be developed within an individual. And I believe that love, compassion, and altruism are the fundamental basis for peace. Once these qualities are developed within an individual, he or she is then able to create an atmosphere of peace and harmony. This atmosphere can be expanded and extended from the individual to his family, from the family to the community and eventually to the whole world.

Peace Is Every Step is a guidebook for a journey in exactly this direction. Thich Nhat Hanh begins by teaching mindfulness of breathing and awareness of the small acts of our daily lives, then shows us how to use the benefits of mindfulness and concentration to transform and heal difficult psychological states. Finally he shows us the connection between personal, inner peace and peace on Earth. This is a very worthwhile book. It can change individual lives and the life of our society.

Editor's Introduction

As I walked slowly and mindfully through a green oak forest this morning, a brilliant red-orange sun rose on the horizon. It immediately evoked for me images of India, where a group of us joined Thich Nhat Hanh the year before last to visit the sites where the Buddha taught. On one walk to a cave near Bodh Gaya, we stopped in a field surrounded by rice paddies and recited this poem:

> *Peace is every step.*
> *The shining red sun is my heart.*
> *Each flower smiles with me.*
> *How green, how fresh all that grows.*
> *How cool the wind blows.*
> *Peace is every step.*
> *It turns the endless path to joy.*

These lines summarize the essence of Thich Nhat Hanh's message—that peace is not external or to be sought after or attained. Living mindfully, slowing down and enjoying each step and each breath, is enough. Peace is already present in each step, and if we walk in this way, a flower will bloom under our feet with every step. In fact the flowers will smile at us and wish us well on our way.

I met Thich Nhat Hanh in 1982 when he attended the Reverence for Life conference in New York. I was one of the first American Buddhists he had met, and it fascinated him that I looked, dressed, and, to some extent, acted like the novices he had trained in Vietnam for two decades. When my teacher, Richard Baker-roshi, invited him to visit our meditation center in San Francisco the following year, he happily accepted, and this began a new phase in the extraordinary life of this gentle monk, whom Baker-roshi characterized as "a cross between a cloud, a snail, and a piece of heavy machinery—a true religious presence."

Thich Nhat Hanh was born in central Vietnam in 1926 and was ordained a Buddhist monk in 1942, at the age of sixteen. Just eight years later, he co-founded what was to become the foremost center of Buddhist studies in South Vietnam, the An Quang Buddhist Institute.

In 1961, Nhat Hanh came to the United States to study and teach comparative religion at Columbia and Princeton Universities. But in 1963, his monk-colleagues in Vietnam telegrammed him to come home to join them in their work to stop the war following the fall of the oppressive Diem regime. He immediately returned and helped lead one of the great nonviolent resistance movements of the century, based entirely on Gandhian principles.

In 1964, along with a group of university professors and students in Vietnam, Thich Nhat Hanh founded the School of Youth for Social Service, called by the American press the "little Peace Corps," in which teams of young people went into the countryside to establish schools and health clinics, and later to rebuild villages that had been bombed. By the time of the fall of Saigon, there were more than 10,000 monks, nuns, and young social workers involved in the work. In the same year, he helped set up what was to become one of the most prestigious publishing houses in Vietnam, La Boi Press. In his books and as editor-in-chief of the official publication of the Unified Buddhist Church, he called for reconciliation between the warring parties in Vietnam, and because of that his writings were censored by both opposing governments.

In 1966, at the urging of his fellow monks, he accepted an invitation from the Fellowship of Reconciliation and Cornell University to come to the U.S. "to describe to [us] the aspirations and the agony of the voiceless masses of the Vietnamese people" (*New Yorker*, June 25, 1966). He had a densely packed schedule of speaking engagements and private meetings, and spoke convincingly in favor of a ceasefire and a negotiated settlement. Martin Luther King, Jr. was so moved by Nhat Hanh and his proposals for peace that he nominated him for the 1967 Nobel Peace Prize, saying, "I know of no one more worthy of the Nobel Peace Prize than this gentle monk from Vietnam." Largely due to Thich Nhat Hanh's influence, King came out publicly against the war at a press conference, with Nhat Hanh, in Chicago.

When Thomas Merton, the well-known Catholic monk and mystic, met Thich Nhat Hanh at his monastery, Gethsemani, near Louisville, Kentucky, he told his students, "Just the way he opens the door and enters a room demonstrates his understanding. He is a true monk." Merton went on to write an essay, "Nhat

Hanh Is My Brother," an impassioned plea to listen to Nhat Hanh's proposals for peace and lend full support for Nhat Hanh's advocacy of peace. After important meetings with Senators Fullbright and Kennedy, Secretary of Defense McNamara, and others in Washington, Thich Nhat Hanh went to Europe, where he met with a number of heads of state and officials of the Catholic church, including two audiences with Pope Paul VI, urging cooperation between Catholics and Buddhists to help bring peace to Vietnam.

In 1969, at the request of the Unified Buddhist Church of Vietnam, Thich Nhat Hanh set up the Buddhist Peace Delegation to the Paris Peace Talks. After the Peace Accords were signed in 1973, he was refused permission to return to Vietnam, and he established a small community a hundred miles southwest of Paris, called "Sweet Potato." In 1976–77, Nhat Hanh conducted an operation to rescue boat people in the Gulf of Siam, but hostility from the governments of Thailand and Singapore made it impossible to continue. So for the following five years, he stayed at Sweet Potato in retreat—meditating, reading, writing, binding books, gardening, and occasionally receiving visitors.

In June 1982, Thich Nhat Hanh visited New York, and later that year established Plum Village, a larger retreat center near Bordeaux, surrounded by vineyards and fields of wheat, corn, and sunflowers. Since 1983 he has travelled to North America every other year to lead retreats and give lectures on mindful living and social responsibility, "making peace right in the moment we are alive."

Although Thich Nhat Hanh cannot visit his homeland, handwritten copies of his books continue to circulate illegally in Vietnam. His presence is also felt through his students and colleagues throughout the world who work full-time trying to relieve the suffering of the desperately poor people of Vietnam, clandestinely supporting hungry families and campaigning on behalf of writers, artists, monks, and nuns who have been imprisoned for their beliefs and their art. This work extends to helping refugees threatened with repatriation, and sending material and spiritual aid to refugees in the camps of Thailand, Malaysia, and Hong Kong.

Now sixty-four years old, yet looking twenty years younger, Thich Nhat Hanh is emerging as one of the great teachers of the twentieth century. In the midst of our society's emphasis on speed, efficiency, and material success, Thich Nhat Hanh's ability to walk calmly with peace and awareness and to teach us to do the same has led to his enthusiastic reception in the West. Although his mode of expression is simple, his message reveals the quintessence of the deep understanding of reality that comes from his meditations, his Buddhist training, and his work in the world.

His way of teaching centers around conscious breathing—the awareness of each breath—and, through conscious breathing, mindfulness of each act of daily life. Meditation, he tells us, is not just in a meditation hall. It is just as sacred to wash the dishes mindfully as to bow deeply or light incense. He also tells us that forming a smile on our face can relax hundreds of muscles in our body—he calls it "mouth yoga"—and in fact, recent studies have shown that when we flex our facial muscles into expressions of joy, we do indeed produce the effects on our nervous system that go with real joy. Peace and happiness are available, he reminds us, if we can only quiet our distracted thinking long enough to come back to the present moment and notice the blue sky, the child's smile, the beautiful sunrise. "If we are peaceful, if we are happy, we can smile, and everyone in our family, our entire society, will benefit from our peace."

Peace Is Every Step is a book of reminders. In the rush of modern life, we tend to lose touch with the peace that is available in each moment. Thich Nhat Hanh's creativity lies in his ability to make use of the very situations that usually pressure and antagonize us. For him, a ringing telephone is a signal to call us back to our true selves. Dirty dishes, red lights, and traffic jams are spiritual friends on the path of mindfulness. The most profound satisfactions, the deepest feelings of joy and completeness lie as close at hand as our next aware breath and the smile we can form right now.

Peace Is Every Step was assembled from Thich Nhat Hanh's lectures, published and unpublished writings, and informal conversations, by a small group of friends—Therese Fitzgerald, Michael Katz, Jane Hirshfield, and myself—working closely with Thây Nhat Hanh (pronounced "tie"—the Vietnamese word for "teacher") and with Leslie Meredith, our attentive, thorough, and sensitive editor at Bantam. Patricia Curtan provided the beautiful dandelion. Special thanks to Marion Tripp, who wrote the "Dandelion Poem."

This book is the clearest and most complete message yet of a great *bodhisattva*, who has dedicated his life to the enlightenment of others. Thich Nhat Hanh's teaching is simultaneously inspirational and very practical. I hope the reader enjoys this book as much as we have enjoyed making it available.

Arnold Kotler
Thenac, France
July 1990

PEACE IS
EVERY STEP

PART ONE

Breathe! You Are Alive

Twenty-Four
Brand-New Hours

Every morning, when we wake up, we have twenty-four brand-new hours to live. What a precious gift! We have the capacity to live in a way that these twenty-four hours will bring peace, joy, and happiness to ourselves and others.

Peace is present right here and now, in ourselves and in everything we do and see. The question is whether or not we are in touch with it. We don't have to travel far away to enjoy the blue sky. We don't have to leave our city or even our neighborhood to enjoy the eyes of a beautiful child. Even the air we breathe can be a source of joy.

We can smile, breathe, walk, and eat our meals in a way that allows us to be in touch with the abundance of happiness that is available. We are very good at preparing to live, but not very good at living. We know how to sacrifice ten years for a diploma, and we are willing to work very hard to get a job, a car, a house, and so on. But we have difficulty remembering that we are alive in the present moment, the only moment there is for us to be alive. Every breath we take, every step we make, can be filled with peace, joy, and serenity. We need only to be awake, alive in the present moment.

This small book is offered as a bell of mindfulness, a reminder that happiness is possible only in the present moment. Of course, planning for the future is a part of life. But even planning can only take place in the present moment. This book is an invitation to come back to the present moment and find peace and joy. I offer some of my experiences and a number of techniques that may be of help. But please do not wait until finishing this book to find peace. Peace and happiness are available in every moment. Peace is every step. We shall walk hand in hand. *Bon voyage.*

The Dandelion Has My Smile

If a child smiles, if an adult smiles, that is very important. If in our daily lives we can smile, if we can be peaceful and happy, not only we, but everyone will profit from it. If we really know how to live, what better way to start the day than with a smile? Our smile affirms our awareness and determination to live in peace and joy. The source of a true smile is an awakened mind.

How can you remember to smile when you wake up? You might hang a reminder—such as a branch, a leaf, a painting, or some inspiring words—in your window or from the ceiling above your bed, so that you notice it when you wake up. Once you develop the practice of smiling, you may not need a reminder. You will smile as soon as you hear a bird singing or see the sunlight streaming through the window. Smiling helps you approach the day with gentleness and understanding.

When I see someone smile, I know immediately that he or she is dwelling in awareness. This half-smile, how many artists have labored to bring it to the lips of countless statues and paintings? I am sure the same smile must have been on the faces of the sculptors and painters as they worked. Can you imagine an angry painter giving birth to such a smile? Mona Lisa's smile is light, just a hint of a smile. Yet even a smile like that is enough to relax all the muscles in our face, to banish all worries and fatigue. A tiny bud of a smile on our lips nourishes awareness and calms us miraculously. It returns to us the peace we thought we had lost.

Our smile will bring happiness to us and to those around us. Even if we spend a lot of money on gifts for everyone in our family, nothing we buy could give them as much happiness as the gift of our awareness, our smile. And this precious gift costs nothing. At the end of a retreat in California, a friend wrote this poem:

> *I have lost my smile,*
> *but don't worry.*
> *The dandelion has it.*

If you have lost your smile and yet are still capable of seeing that a dandelion is keeping it for you, the situation is not too bad. You still have enough mindfulness to see that the smile is there.

You only need to breathe consciously one or two times and you will recover your smile. The dandelion is one member of your community of friends. It is there, quite faithful, keeping your smile for you.

In fact, everything around you is keeping your smile for you. You don't need to feel isolated. You only have to open yourself to the support that is all around you, and in you. Like the friend who saw that her smile was being kept by the dandelion, you can breathe in awareness, and your smile will return.

Conscious Breathing

There are a number of breathing techniques you can use to make life vivid and more enjoyable. The first exercise is very simple. As you breathe in, you say to yourself, "Breathing in, I know that I am breathing in." And as you breathe out, say, "Breathing out, I know that I am breathing out." Just that. You recognize your in-breath as an in-breath and your out-breath as an out-breath. You don't even need to recite the whole sentence; you can use just two words: "In" and "Out." This technique can help you keep your mind on your breath. As you practice, your breath will become peaceful and gentle, and your mind and body will also become peaceful and gentle. This is not a difficult exercise. In just a few minutes you can realize the fruit of meditation.

Breathing in and out is very important, and it is enjoyable. Our breathing is the link between our body and our mind. Sometimes our mind is thinking of one thing and our body is doing another, and mind and body are not unified. By concentrating on our breathing, "In" and "Out," we bring body and mind back together, and become whole again. Conscious breathing is an important bridge.

To me, breathing is a joy that I cannot miss. Every day, I practice conscious breathing, and in my small meditation room, I have calligraphed this sentence: "Breathe, you are alive!" Just breathing and smiling can make us very happy, because when we breathe consciously we recover ourselves completely and encounter life in the present moment.

Present Moment, Wonderful Moment

In our busy society, it is a great fortune to breathe consciously from time to time. We can practice conscious breathing not only while sitting in a meditation room, but also while working at the office or at home, while driving our car, or sitting on a bus, wherever we are, at any time throughout the day.

There are so many exercises we can do to help us breathe consciously. Besides the simple "In-Out" exercise, we can recite these four lines silently as we breathe in and out:

> *Breathing in, I calm my body.*
> *Breathing out, I smile.*
> *Dwelling in the present moment,*
> *I know this is a wonderful moment!*

"Breathing in, I calm my body." Reciting this line is like drinking a glass of cool lemonade on a hot day—you can feel the coolness permeate your body. When I breathe in and recite this line, I actually feel my breath calming my body and mind.

"Breathing out, I smile." You know a smile can relax hundreds of muscles in your face. Wearing a smile on your face is a sign that you are master of yourself.

"Dwelling in the present moment." While I sit here, I don't think of anything else. I sit here, and I know exactly where I am.

"I know this is a wonderful moment." It is a joy to sit, stable and at ease, and return to our breathing, our smiling, our true nature. Our appointment with life is in the present moment. If we do not have peace and joy right now, when will we have peace and joy—tomorrow, or after tomorrow? What is preventing us from being happy right now? As we follow our breathing, we can say, simply, "Calming, Smiling, Present moment, Wonderful moment."

This exercise is not just for beginners. Many of us who have practiced meditation and conscious breathing for forty or fifty years continue to practice in this same way, because this kind of exercise is so important and so easy.

Thinking Less

While we practice conscious breathing, our thinking will slow down, and we can give ourselves a real rest. Most of the time, we think too much, and mindful breathing helps us to be calm, relaxed, and peaceful. It helps us stop thinking so much and stop being possessed by sorrows of the past and worries about the future. It enables us to be in touch with life, which is wonderful in the present moment.

Of course, thinking is important, but quite a lot of our thinking is useless. It is as if, in our head, each of us has a cassette tape that is always running, day and night. We think of this and we think of that, and it is difficult to stop. With a cassette, we can just press the stop button. But with our thinking, we do not have any button. We may think and worry so much that we cannot sleep. If we go to the doctor for some sleeping pills or tranquilizers, these may make the situation worse, because we do not really rest during that kind of sleep, and if we continue using these drugs, we may become addicted. We continue to live tensely, and we may have nightmares.

According to the method of conscious breathing, when we breathe in and out, we stop thinking, because saying "In" and "Out" is not thinking—"In" and "Out" are only words to help us concentrate on our breathing. If we keep breathing in and out this way for a few minutes, we become quite refreshed. We recover ourselves, and we can encounter the beautiful things around us in the present moment. The past is gone, the future is not yet here. If we do not go back to ourselves in the present moment, we cannot be in touch with life.

When we are in touch with the refreshing, peaceful, and healing elements within ourselves and around us, we learn how to cherish and protect these things and make them grow. These elements of peace are available to us anytime.

Nourishing Awareness
in Each Moment

One cold, winter evening I returned home from a walk in the hills, and I found that all the doors and windows in my hermitage had blown open. When I had left earlier, I hadn't secured them, and a cold wind had blown through the house, opened the windows, and scattered the papers from my desk all over the room. Immediately, I closed the doors and windows, lit a lamp, picked up the papers, and arranged them neatly on my desk. Then I started a fire in the fireplace, and soon the crackling logs brought warmth back to the room.

Sometimes in a crowd we feel tired, cold, and lonely. We may wish to withdraw to be by ourselves and become warm again, as I did when I closed the windows and sat by the fire, protected from the damp, cold wind. Our senses are our windows to the world, and sometimes the wind blows through them and disturbs everything within us. Some of us leave our windows open all the time, allowing the sights and sounds of the world to invade us, penetrate us, and expose our sad, troubled selves. We feel so cold, lonely, and afraid. Do you ever find yourself watching an awful TV program, unable to turn it off? The raucous noises, explosions of gunfire, are upsetting. Yet you don't get up and turn it off. Why do you torture yourself in this way? Don't you want to close your windows? Are you frightened of solitude—the emptiness and the loneliness you may find when you face yourself alone?

Watching a bad TV program, we *become* the TV program. We are what we feel and perceive. If we are angry, we are the anger. If we are in love, we are love. If we look at a snow-covered mountain peak, we are the mountain. We can be anything we want, so why do we open our windows to bad TV programs made by sensationalist producers in search of easy money, programs that make our hearts pound, our fists tighten, and leave us exhausted? Who allows such TV programs to be made and seen by even the very young? We do! We are too undemanding, too ready to watch whatever is on the screen, too lonely, lazy, or bored to create our own lives. We turn on the TV and leave it on, allowing someone else to guide us, shape us, and destroy us. Losing ourselves in this way is leaving our fate in the hands of others who may not be acting responsibly. We must be aware of which programs do harm to our nervous systems, minds, and hearts, and which programs benefit us.

Of course, I am not talking only about television. All around us, how many lures are set by our fellows and ourselves? In a single day, how many times do we become lost and scattered because of them? We must be very careful to protect our fate and our peace. I am not suggesting that we just shut all our windows, for there are many miracles in the world we call "outside." We can open our windows to these miracles and look at any one of them with awareness. This way, even while sitting beside a clear, flowing stream, listening to beautiful music, or watching an excellent movie, we need not lose ourselves entirely in the stream, the music, or the film. We can continue to be aware of ourselves and our breathing. With the sun of awareness shining in us, we can avoid most dangers. The stream will be purer, the music more harmonious, and the soul of the filmmaker completely visible.

As beginning meditators, we may want to leave the city and go off to the countryside to help close those windows that trouble our spirit. There we can become one with the quiet forest, and rediscover and restore ourselves, without being swept away by the chaos of the "outside world." The fresh and silent woods help us remain in awareness, and when our awareness is well-rooted and we can maintain it without faltering, we may wish to return to the city and remain there, less troubled. But sometimes we cannot leave the city, and we have to find the refreshing and peaceful elements that can heal us right in the midst of our busy lives. We may wish to visit a good friend who can comfort us, or go for a walk in a park and enjoy the trees and the cool breeze. Whether we are in the city, the countryside, or the wilderness, we need to sustain ourselves by choosing our surroundings carefully and nourishing our awareness in each moment.

Sitting Anywhere

When you need to slow down and come back to yourself, you do not need to rush home to your meditation cushion or to a meditation center in order to practice conscious breathing. You can breathe anywhere, just sitting on your chair at the office or sitting in your automobile. Even if you are at a shopping center filled with people or waiting in line at a bank, if you begin to feel depleted and need to return to yourself, you can practice conscious breathing and smiling just standing there.

Wherever you are, you can breathe mindfully. We all need to go back to ourselves from time to time, in order to be able to confront the difficulties of life. We can do this in any position—standing, sitting, lying down, or walking. If you can sit down, however, the sitting position is the most stable.

One time, I was waiting for a plane that was four hours late at Kennedy Airport in New York, and I enjoyed sitting cross-legged right in the waiting area. I just rolled up my sweater and used it as a cushion, and I sat. People looked at me curiously, but after a while they ignored me, and I sat in peace. There was no place to rest, the airport was full of people, so I just made myself comfortable where I was. You may not want to meditate so conspicuously, but breathing mindfully in any position at any time can help you recover yourself.

Sitting Meditation

The most stable posture for meditation is sitting cross-legged on a cushion. Choose a cushion that is the right thickness to support you. The half-lotus and full-lotus positions are excellent for establishing stability of body and mind. To sit in the lotus position, gently cross your legs by placing one foot (for the half-lotus) or both feet (for the full-lotus) on the opposite thighs. If the lotus position is difficult, it is fine just to sit cross-legged or in any comfortable position. Allow your back to be straight, keep your eyes half closed, and fold your hands comfortably on your lap. If you prefer, you can sit in a chair with your feet flat on the floor and your hands resting on your lap. Or you can lie on the floor, on your back, with your legs straight out, a few inches apart, and your arms at your sides, preferably palms up.

If your legs or feet fall asleep or begin to hurt during sitting meditation so that your concentration becomes disturbed, feel free to adjust your position. If you do this slowly and attentively, following your breathing and each movement of your body, you will not lose a single moment of concentration. If the pain is severe, stand up, walk slowly and mindfully, and when you are ready, sit down again.

In some meditation centers, practitioners are not permitted to move during periods of sitting meditation. They often have to endure great discomfort. To me, this seems unnatural. When a part of our body is numb or in pain, it is telling us something, and we should listen to it. We sit in meditation to help us cultivate peace, joy, and nonviolence, not to endure physical strain or to injure our bodies. To change the position of our feet or do a little walking meditation will not disturb others very much, and it can help us a lot.

Sometimes, we can use meditation as a way of hiding from ourselves and from life, like a rabbit going back to his hole. Doing this, we may be able to avoid some problems for a while, but when we leave our "hole," we will have to confront them again. For example, if we practice our meditation very intensely, we may feel a kind of relief as we exhaust ourselves and divert our energy from confronting our difficulties. But when our energy returns, our problems will return with them.

We need to practice meditation gently, but steadily, throughout daily life, not wasting a single opportunity or event to see deeply into the true nature of life, including our everyday problems. Practicing in this way, we dwell in profound communion with life.

Bells of Mindfulness

In my tradition, we use the temple bells to remind us to come back to the present moment. Every time we hear the bell, we stop talking, stop our thinking, and return to ourselves, breathing in and out, and smiling. Whatever we are doing, we pause for a moment and just enjoy our breathing. Sometimes we also recite this verse:

> *Listen, listen.*
> *This wonderful sound brings me back to my true self.*

When we breathe in, we say, "Listen, listen," and when we breathe out, we say, "This wonderful sound brings me back to my true self."

Since I have come to the West, I have not heard many Buddhist temple bells. But fortunately, there are church bells all over Europe. There do not seem to be as many in the United States; I think that is a pity. Whenever I give a lecture in Switzerland, I always make use of the church bells to practice mindfulness. When the bell rings, I stop talking, and all of us listen to the full sound of the bell. We enjoy it so much. (I think it is better than the lecture!) When we hear the bell, we can pause and enjoy our breathing and get in touch with the wonders of life that are around us—the flowers, the children, the beautiful sounds. Every time we get back in touch with ourselves, the conditions become favorable for us to encounter life in the present moment.

One day in Berkeley, I proposed to professors and students at the University of California that every time the bell on the campus sounds, the professors and students should pause in order to breathe consciously. Everyone should take the time to enjoy being alive! We should not just be rushing around all day. We have to learn to really enjoy our church bells and our school bells. Bells are beautiful, and they can wake us up.

If you have a bell at home, you can practice breathing and smiling with its lovely sound. But you do not have to carry a bell into your office or factory. You can use any sound to remind you to pause, breathe in and out, and enjoy the present moment. The buzzer that goes off when you forget to fasten the seat belt in your car is a bell of mindfulness. Even non-sounds, such as the rays of sunlight coming through the window, are bells of mindfulness that can remind us to return to ourselves, breathe, smile, and live fully in the present moment.

Cookie of Childhood

When I was four years old, my mother used to bring me a cookie every time she came home from the market. I always went to the front yard and took my time eating it, sometimes half an hour or forty-five minutes for one cookie. I would take a small bite and look up at the sky. Then I would touch the dog with my feet and take another small bite. I just enjoyed being there, with the sky, the earth, the bamboo thickets, the cat, the dog, the flowers. I was able to do that because I did not have much to worry about. I did not think of the future, I did not regret the past. I was entirely in the present moment, with my cookie, the dog, the bamboo thickets, the cat, and everything.

It is possible to eat our meals as slowly and joyfully as I ate the cookie of my childhood. Maybe you have the impression that you have lost the cookie of your childhood, but I am sure it is still there, somewhere in your heart. Everything is still there, and if you really want it, you can find it. Eating mindfully is a most im-

portant practice of meditation. We can eat in a way that we restore the cookie of our childhood. The present moment is filled
with joy and happiness. If you are attentive, you will see it.

Tangerine Meditation

If I offer you a freshly picked tangerine to enjoy, I think the degree to which you enjoy it will depend on your mindfulness. If
you are free of worries and anxiety, you will enjoy it more. If you
are possessed by anger or fear, the tangerine may not be very real
to you.

One day, I offered a number of children a basket filled with
tangerines. The basket was passed around, and each child took
one tangerine and put it in his or her palm. We each looked at our
tangerine, and the children were invited to meditate on its
origins. They saw not only their tangerine, but also its mother,
the tangerine tree. With some guidance, they began to visualize
the blossoms in the sunshine and in the rain. Then they saw pet-
als falling down and the tiny green fruit appear. The sunshine
and the rain continued, and the tiny tangerine grew. Now someone has picked it, and the tangerine is here. After seeing this, each
child was invited to peel the tangerine slowly, noticing the mist
and the fragrance of the tangerine, and then bring it up to his or

her mouth and have a mindful bite, in full awareness of the texture and taste of the fruit and the juice coming out. We ate slowly like that.

Each time you look at a tangerine, you can see deeply into it. You can see everything in the universe in one tangerine. When you peel it and smell it, it's wonderful. You can take your time eating a tangerine and be very happy.

The Eucharist

The practice of the Eucharist is a practice of awareness. When Jesus broke the bread and shared it with his disciples, he said, "Eat this. This is my flesh." He knew that if his disciples would eat one piece of bread in mindfulness, they would have real life. In their daily lives, they may have eaten their bread in forgetfulness, so the bread was not bread at all; it was a ghost. In our daily lives, we may see the people around us, but if we lack mindfulness, they are just phantoms, not real people, and we ourselves are also ghosts. Practicing mindfulness enables us to become a real person. When we are a real person, we see real people around us, and life is present in all its richness. The practice of eating bread, a tangerine, or a cookie is the same.

When we breathe, when we are mindful, when we look

deeply at our food, life becomes real at that very moment. To me, the rite of the Eucharist is a wonderful practice of mindfulness. In a drastic way, Jesus tried to wake up his disciples.

Eating Mindfully

A few years ago, I asked some children, "What is the purpose of eating breakfast?" One boy replied, "To get energy for the day." Another said, "The purpose of eating breakfast is to eat breakfast." I think the second child is more correct. The purpose of eating is to eat.

Eating a meal in mindfulness is an important practice. We turn off the TV, put down our newspaper, and work together for five or ten minutes, setting the table and finishing whatever needs to be done. During these few minutes, we can be very happy. When the food is on the table and everyone is seated, we practice breathing: "Breathing in, I calm my body. Breathing out, I smile," three times. We can recover ourselves completely after three breaths like this.

Then, we look at each person as we breathe in and out in order to be in touch with ourselves and everyone at the table. We don't need two hours to see another person. If we are really settled within ourselves, we only need to look for one or two seconds, and that is enough to see. I think that if a family has five members, only about five or ten seconds are needed to practice this "looking and seeing."

After breathing, we smile. Sitting at the table with other people, we have a chance to offer an authentic smile of friendship and understanding. It is very easy, but not many people do it. To me, this is the most important practice. We look at each person and smile at him or her. Breathing and smiling together is a very important practice. If the people in a household cannot smile at each other, the situation is very dangerous.

After breathing and smiling, we look down at the food in a way that allows the food to become real. This food reveals our connection with the earth. Each bite contains the life of the sun and the earth. The extent to which our food reveals itself depends on us. We can see and taste the whole universe in a piece of bread! Contemplating our food for a few seconds before eating, and eating in mindfulness, can bring us much happiness.

Having the opportunity to sit with our family and friends and enjoy wonderful food is something precious, something not everyone has. Many people in the world are hungry. When I hold a bowl of rice or a piece of bread, I know that I am fortunate, and I feel compassion for all those who have no food to eat and are without friends or family. This is a very deep practice. We do not need to go to a temple or a church in order to practice this. We can practice it right at our dinner table. Mindful eating can cultivate seeds of compassion and understanding that will strengthen us to do something to help hungry and lonely people be nourished.

In order to aid mindfulness during meals, you may like to eat silently from time to time. Your first silent meal may cause you to feel a little uncomfortable, but once you become used to it, you will realize that meals in silence bring much peace and happiness. Just as we turn off the TV before eating, we can "turn off" the talking in order to enjoy the food and the presence of one another.

I do not recommend silent meals every day. Talking to each other can be a wonderful way to be together in mindfulness. But we have to distinguish among different kinds of talk. Some subjects can separate us: for instance, if we talk about other people's shortcomings. The carefully prepared food will have no value if we let this kind of talk dominate our meal. When instead we speak about things that nourish our awareness of the food and our being together, we cultivate the kind of happiness that is necessary for us to grow. If we compare this experience with the experience of talking about other people's shortcomings, we will realize that the awareness of the piece of bread in our mouth is much more nourishing. It brings life in and makes life real.

So, while eating, we should refrain from discussing subjects that can destroy our awareness of our family and the food. But we should feel free to say things that can nourish awareness and happiness. For instance, if there is a dish that you like very much, you can notice if other people are also enjoying it, and if one of them is not, you can help him or her appreciate the wonderful dish prepared with loving care. If someone is thinking about something other than the good food on the table, such as his difficulties in the office or with friends, he is losing the present moment and the food. You can say, "This dish is wonderful, don't you agree?" to draw him out of his thinking and worries and bring him back to the here and now, enjoying you, enjoying the wonderful dish. You become a *bodhisattva*, helping a living being become enlightened. Children, in particular, are very capable of practicing mindfulness and reminding others to do the same.

Washing Dishes

To my mind, the idea that doing dishes is unpleasant can occur only when you aren't doing them. Once you are standing in front of the sink with your sleeves rolled up and your hands in the warm water, it is really quite pleasant. I enjoy taking my time with each dish, being fully aware of the dish, the water, and each movement of my hands. I know that if I hurry in order to eat dessert sooner, the time of washing dishes will be unpleasant and not worth living. That would be a pity, for each minute, each second of life is a miracle. The dishes themselves and the fact that I am here washing them are miracles!

If I am incapable of washing dishes joyfully, if I want to finish them quickly so I can go and have dessert, I will be equally incapable of enjoying my dessert. With the fork in my hand, I will be thinking about what to do next, and the texture and the flavor of the dessert, together with the pleasure of eating it, will be lost. I will always be dragged into the future, never able to live in the present moment.

Each thought, each action in the sunlight of awareness becomes sacred. In this light, no boundary exists between the sacred and the profane. I must confess it takes me a bit longer to do the dishes, but I live fully in every moment, and I am happy. Washing the dishes is at the same time a means and an end—that is, not only do we do the dishes in order to have clean dishes, we also do the dishes just to do the dishes, to live fully in each moment while washing them.

Walking Meditation

Walking meditation can be very enjoyable. We walk slowly, alone or with friends, if possible in some beautiful place. Walking meditation is really to enjoy the walking—walking not in order to arrive, but just to walk. The purpose is to be in the present moment and, aware of our breathing and our walking, to enjoy each step. Therefore we have to shake off all worries and anxieties, not thinking of the future, not thinking of the past, just enjoying the present moment. We can take the hand of a child as we do it. We walk, we make steps as if we are the happiest person on Earth.

Although we walk all the time, our walking is usually more like running. When we walk like that, we print anxiety and sorrow on the Earth. We have to walk in a way that we only print peace and serenity on the Earth. We can all do this, provided that we want it very much. Any child can do it. If we can take one step like this, we can take two, three, four, and five. When we are able to take one step peacefully and happily, we are working for the cause of peace and happiness for the whole of humankind. Walking meditation is a wonderful practice.

When we do walking meditation outside, we walk a little slower than our normal pace, and we coordinate our breathing with our steps. For example, we may take three steps with each in-breath and three steps with each out-breath. So we can say, "In, in, in. Out, out, out." "In" is to help us to identify the in-breath. Every time we call something by its name, we make it more real, like saying the name of a friend.

If your lungs want four steps instead of three, please give them four steps. If they want only two steps, give them two. The lengths of your in-breath and out-breath do not have to be the same. For example, you can take three steps with each inhalation and four with each exhalation. If you feel happy, peaceful, and joyful while you are walking, you are practicing correctly.

Be aware of the contact between your feet and the Earth. Walk as if you are kissing the Earth with your feet. We have caused a lot of damage to the Earth. Now it is time for us to take good care of her. We bring our peace and calm to the surface of the Earth and share the lesson of love. We walk in that spirit. From time to time, when we see something beautiful, we may want to stop and look at it—a tree, a flower, some children playing. As we look, we continue to follow our breathing, lest we lose the beautiful flower and get caught up in our thoughts. When we want to resume walking, we just start again. Each step we take will create a cool breeze, refreshing our body and mind. Every step makes a flower bloom under our feet. We can do it only if we do not think of the future or the past, if we know that life can only be found in the present moment.

Telephone Meditation

The telephone is very convenient, but we can be tyrannized by it. We may find its ring disturbing or feel interrupted by too many calls. When we talk on the phone, we may forget that we are talking on the telephone, wasting precious time (and money). Often we talk about things that are not that important. How many times have we received our phone bill and winced at the amount of it? The telephone bell creates in us a kind of vibration, and maybe some anxiety: "Who is calling? Is it good news or bad news?" Yet some force in us pulls us to the phone, and we cannot resist. We are victims of our own telephone.

I recommend that the next time you hear the phone ring, just stay where you are, breathe in and out consciously, smile to yourself, and recite this verse: "Listen, listen. This wonderful sound brings me back to my true self." When the bell rings for the second time, you can repeat the verse, and your smile will be even more solid. When you smile, the muscles of your face relax, and your tension quickly vanishes. You can afford to practice breathing and smiling like this, because if the person calling has something important to say, she will certainly wait for at least three rings. When the phone rings for the third time, you can continue to practice breathing and smiling, as you walk to the phone slowly, with all your sovereignty. You are your own master. You know that you are smiling not only for your own sake, but also for the sake of the other person. If you are irritated or angry, the other person will receive your negativity. But because you have been breathing consciously and smiling, you are dwelling in mindfulness, and when you pick up the phone, how fortunate for the person calling you!

Before making a phone call, you can also breathe in and out three times, then dial. When you hear the other phone ring, you know that your friend is practicing breathing and smiling and will not pick it up until the third ring. So you tell yourself, "She is breathing, why not me?" You practice breathing in and out, and she does too. That's very beautiful!

You don't have to go into a meditation hall to do this wonderful practice of meditation. You can do it in your office and at home. I don't know how phone operators can practice while so many phones ring simultaneously. I rely on you to find a way for operators to practice telephone meditation. But those of us who are not operators have the right to three breaths. Practicing telephone meditation can counteract stress and depression and bring mindfulness into our daily lives.

Driving Meditation

In Vietnam, forty years ago, I was the first monk to ride a bicycle. At that time, it was not considered a very "monkish" thing to do. But today, monks ride motorcycles and drive cars. We have to keep our meditation practices up to date and respond to the real situation in the world, so I have written a simple verse you can recite before starting your car. I hope you find it helpful:

Before starting the car,
I know where I am going.
The car and I are one.
If the car goes fast, I go fast.

Sometimes we don't really need to use the car, but because we want to get away from ourselves, we go for a drive. We feel that there is a vacuum in us and we don't want to confront it. We don't like being so busy, but every time we have a spare moment, we are afraid of being alone with ourselves. We want to escape. Either we turn on the television, pick up the telephone, read a novel, go out with a friend, or take the car and go somewhere. Our civilization teaches us to act this way and provides us with many things we can use to lose touch with ourselves. If we recite this poem as we are about to turn the ignition key of our car, it can be like a torch, and we may see that we don't need to go anywhere. Wherever we go, our "self" will be with us; we cannot escape. So it may be better, and more pleasant, to leave the engine off and go out for a walking meditation.

It is said that in the last several years, two million square miles of forest land have been destroyed by acid rain, partly because of our cars. "Before starting the car, I know where I am going," is a very deep question. Where shall we go? To our own destruction? If the trees die, we humans are going to die also. If the journey you are making is necessary, please do not hesitate to go. But if you see that it is not really important, you can remove the key from the ignition and go instead for a walk along the riverbank or through a park. You will return to yourself and make friends with the trees again.

"The car and I are one." We have the impression that we are the boss, and the car is only an instrument, but that is not true. When we use any instrument or machine, we change. A violinist with his violin becomes very beautiful. A man with a gun becomes very dangerous. When we use a car, we are ourselves *and* the car.

Driving is a daily task in this society. I am not suggesting you stop driving, just that you do so consciously. While we are driving, we think only about arriving. Therefore, every time we see a red light, we are not very happy. The red light is a kind of enemy that prevents us from attaining our goal. But we can also see the red light as a bell of mindfulness, reminding us to return to the present moment. The next time you see a red light, please smile at it and go back to your breathing. "Breathing in, I calm my body. Breathing out, I smile." It is easy to transform a feeling of irritation into a pleasant feeling. Although it is the same red light, it becomes different. It becomes a friend, helping us remember that it is only in the present moment that we can live our lives.

When I was in Montreal several years ago to lead a retreat, a friend drove me across the city to go to the mountains. I noticed that every time a car stopped in front of me, the sentence "*Je me souviens*" was on the license plate. It means "I remember." I was not sure what they wanted to remember, perhaps their French origins, but I told my friend that I had a gift for him. "Every time you see a car with that sentence, '*Je me souviens*,' remember to breathe and smile. It is a bell of mindfulness. You will have many opportunities to breathe and smile as you drive through Montreal."

He was delighted, and he shared the practice with his friends. Later, when he visited me in France, he told me that it was more difficult to practice in Paris than in Montreal, because in Paris, there is no "*Je me souviens*." I told him, "There are red lights and stop signs everywhere in Paris. Why don't you practice with them?" After he went back to Montreal, through Paris, he wrote me a very nice letter: "Thây, it was very easy to practice in Paris. Every time a car stopped in front of me, I saw the eyes of the

Buddha blinking at me. I had to answer him by breathing and smiling, there was no better answer than that. I had a wonderful time driving in Paris."

The next time you are caught in a traffic jam, don't fight. It's useless to fight. Sit back and smile to yourself, a smile of compassion and loving kindness. Enjoy the present moment, breathing and smiling, and make the other people in your car happy. Happiness is there if you know how to breathe and smile, because happiness can always be found in the present moment. Practicing meditation is to go back to the present moment in order to encounter the flower, the blue sky, the child. Happiness is available.

Decompartmentalization

We have so many compartments in our lives. How can we bring meditation out of the meditation hall and into the kitchen, and the office? In the meditation hall we sit quietly, and try to be aware of each breath. How can our sitting influence our non-sitting time? When a doctor gives you an injection, not only your arm but your whole body benefits from it. When you practice half an hour of sitting meditation a day, that time should be for all twenty-four hours, and not just for that half-hour. One smile, one breath, should be for the benefit of the whole day, not just for that moment. We must practice in a way that removes the barrier between practice and non-practice.

When we walk in the meditation hall, we make careful steps, very slowly. But when we go to the airport or the supermarket, we become quite another person. We walk very quickly, less mindfully. How can we practice mindfulness at the airport and in the supermarket? I have a friend who breathes between telephone calls, and it helps her very much. Another friend does walking meditation between business appointments, walking mindfully between buildings in downtown Denver. Passersby smile at him, and his meetings, even with difficult persons, often turn out to be quite pleasant, and very successful.

We should be able to bring the practice from the meditation hall into our daily lives. We need to discuss among ourselves how to do it. Do you practice breathing between phone calls? Do you practice smiling while cutting carrots? Do you practice relaxation after hours of hard work? These are practical questions. If you know how to apply meditation to dinner time, leisure time, sleeping time, it will penetrate your daily life, and it will also have a tremendous effect on social concerns. Mindfulness can penetrate the activities of everyday life, each minute, each hour of our daily life, and not just be a description of something far away.

Breathing and Scything

Have you ever cut grass with a scythe? Not many people do these days. About ten years ago, I brought a scythe home and tried to cut the grass around my cottage with it. It took more than a week before I found the best way to use it. The way you stand, the way you hold the scythe, the angle of the blade on the grass are all important. I found that if I coordinated the movement of my arms with the rhythm of my breathing, and worked unhurriedly while maintaining awareness of my activity, I was able to work for a longer period of time. When I didn't do this, I became tired in just ten minutes.

During the past few years I have avoided tiring myself and losing my breath. I must take care of my body, treat it with respect as a musician does his instrument. I apply nonviolence to my body, for it is not merely a tool to accomplish something. It itself is the end. I treat my scythe in the same way. As I use it while following my breathing, I feel that my scythe and I breathe together in rhythm. It is true for many other tools as well.

One day an elderly man was visiting my neighbor, and he offered to show me how to use the scythe. He was much more adept than I, but for the most part he used the same position and movements. What surprised me was that he too coordinated his movements with his breathing. Since then, whenever I see anyone cutting his grass with a scythe, I know he is practicing awareness.

Aimlessness

In the West, we are very goal oriented. We know where we want to go, and we are very directed in getting there. This may be useful, but often we forget to enjoy ourselves along the route.

There is a word in Buddhism that means "wishlessness" or "aimlessness." The idea is that you do not put something in front of you and run after it, because everything is already here, in yourself. While we practice walking meditation, we do not try to arrive anywhere. We only make peaceful, happy steps. If we keep thinking of the future, of what we want to realize, we will lose our steps. The same is true with sitting meditation. We sit just to enjoy our sitting; we do not sit in order to attain any goal. This is quite important. Each moment of sitting meditation brings us back to life, and we should sit in a way that we enjoy our sitting for the entire time we do it. Whether we are eating a tangerine, drinking a cup of tea, or walking in meditation, we should do it in a way that is "aimless."

Often we tell ourselves, "Don't just sit there, do something!" But when we practice awareness, we discover something unusual. We discover that the opposite may be more helpful: "Don't just do something, sit there!" We must learn to stop from time to time in order to see clearly. At first, "stopping" may look like a kind of resistance to modern life, but it is not. It is not just a reaction; it is a way of life. Humankind's survival depends on our ability to stop rushing. We have more than 50,000 nuclear bombs, and yet we cannot stop making more. "Stopping" is not only to stop the negative, but to allow positive healing to take place. That is the purpose of our practice—not to avoid life, but to experience and demonstrate that happiness in life is possible now and also in the future.

The foundation of happiness is mindfulness. The basic condition for being happy is our consciousness of being happy. If we are not aware that we are happy, we are not really happy. When we have a toothache, we know that not having a toothache is a wonderful thing. But when we do not have a toothache, we are still not happy. A non-toothache is very pleasant. There are so many things that are enjoyable, but when we don't practice mindfulness, we don't appreciate them. When we practice mindfulness, we come to cherish these things and we learn how to protect them. By taking good care of the present moment, we take good care of the future. Working for peace in the future is to work for peace in the present moment.

Our Life Is
a Work of Art

After a retreat in southern California, an artist asked me, "What is the way to look at a flower so that I can make the most of it for my art?" I said, "If you look in that way, you cannot be in touch with the flower. Abandon all your projects so you can be with the flower with no intention of exploiting it or getting something from it." The same artist told me, "When I am with a friend, I want to profit from him or her." Of course we can profit from a friend, but a friend is more than a source of profit. Just to be with a friend, without thinking to ask for his or her support, help, or advice, is an art.

It has become a kind of habit to look at things with the intention of getting something. We call it "pragmatism," and we say that the truth is something that pays. If we meditate in order to get to the truth, it seems we will be well paid. In meditation, we stop, and we look deeply. We stop just to be there, to be with ourselves and with the world. When we are capable of stopping, we begin to see and, if we can see, we understand. Peace and happiness are the fruit of this process. We should master the art of stopping in order to really be with our friend and with the flower.

How can we bring elements of peace to a society that is very used to making profit? How can our smile be the source of joy and not just a diplomatic maneuver? When we smile to ourselves, that smile is not diplomacy; it is the proof that we are ourselves, that we have full sovereignty over ourselves. Can we write a poem on stopping, aimlessness, or just being? Can we paint something about it? Everything we do is an act of poetry or a painting if we do it with mindfulness. Growing lettuce is poetry. Walking to the supermarket can be a painting.

When we do not trouble ourselves about whether or not something is a work of art, if we just act in each moment with composure and mindfulness, each minute of our life is a work of art. Even when we are not painting or writing, we are still creating. We are pregnant with beauty, joy, and peace, and we are making life more beautiful for many people. Sometimes it is better not to talk about art by using the word "art." If we just act with awareness and integrity, our art will flower, and we don't have to talk about it at all. When we know how to *be* peace, we find that art is a wonderful way to share our peacefulness. Artistic expression will take place in one way or another, but the *being* is essential. So we must go back to ourselves, and when we have joy and peace in ourselves, our creations of art will be quite natural, and they will serve the world in a positive way.

Hope as an Obstacle

Hope is important, because it can make the present moment less difficult to bear. If we believe that tomorrow will be better, we can bear a hardship today. But that is the most that hope can do for us—to make some hardship lighter. When I think deeply about the nature of hope, I see something tragic. Since we cling to our hope in the future, we do not focus our energies and capabilities on the present moment. We use hope to believe something better will happen in the future, that we will arrive at peace, or the Kingdom of God. Hope becomes a kind of obstacle. If you can refrain from hoping, you can bring yourself entirely into the present moment and discover the joy that is already here.

Enlightenment, peace, and joy will not be granted by someone else. The well is within us, and if we dig deeply in the present moment, the water will spring forth. We must go back to the present moment in order to be really alive. When we practice conscious breathing, we practice going back to the present moment where everything is happening.

Western civilization places so much emphasis on the idea of hope that we sacrifice the present moment. Hope is for the future. It cannot help us discover joy, peace, or enlightenment in the present moment. Many religions are based on the notion of hope, and this teaching about refraining from hope may create a strong reaction. But the shock can bring about something important. I do not mean that you should not have hope, but that hope is not enough. Hope can create an obstacle for you, and if you dwell in the energy of hope, you will not bring yourself back entirely into the present moment. If you re-channel those energies into being aware of what is going on in the present moment, you will be able to make a breakthrough and discover joy and peace right in the present moment, inside of yourself and all around you.

A. J. Muste, the mid-twentieth-century leader of the peace movement in America who inspired millions of people, said, "There is no way to peace, peace is the way." This means that we can realize peace right in the present moment with our look, our smile, our words, and our actions. Peace work is not a means. Each step we make should be peace. Each step we make should be joy. Each step we make should be happiness. If we are determined, we can do it. We don't need the future. We can smile and relax. Everything we want is right here in the present moment.

Flower Insights

There is a story about a flower which is well known in the Zen circles. One day the Buddha held up a flower in front of an audience of 1,250 monks and nuns. He did not say anything for quite a long time. The audience was perfectly silent. Everyone seemed to be thinking hard, trying to see the meaning behind the Buddha's gesture. Then, suddenly, the Buddha smiled. He smiled because someone in the audience smiled at him and at the flower. The name of that monk was Mahakashyapa. He was the only person who smiled, and the Buddha smiled back and said, "I have a treasure of insight, and I have transmitted it to Mahakashyapa." That story has been discussed by many generations of Zen students, and people continue to look for its meaning. To me the meaning is quite simple. When someone holds up a flower and shows it to you, he wants you to see it. If you keep thinking, you miss the flower. The person who was not thinking, who was just himself, was able to encounter the flower in depth, and he smiled.

That is the problem of life. If we are not fully ourselves, truly in the present moment, we miss everything. When a child presents himself to you with his smile, if you are not really there— thinking about the future or the past, or preoccupied with other problems—then the child is not really there for you. The technique of being alive is to go back to yourself in order for the child to appear like a marvelous reality. Then you can see him smile and you can embrace him in your arms.

I would like to share a poem with you, written by a friend of mine who died at the age of twenty-eight in Saigon, about thirty years ago. After he died, people found many beautiful poems he had written, and I was startled when I read this poem. It has just a few short lines, but it is very beautiful:

Standing quietly by the fence,
you smile your wondrous smile.
I am speechless, and my senses are filled
by the sounds of your beautiful song,
beginningless and endless.
I bow deeply to you.

"You" refers to a flower, a dahlia. That morning as he passed by a fence, he saw that little flower very deeply and, struck by the sight of it, he stopped and wrote that poem.

I enjoy this poem very much. You might think that the poet was a mystic, because his way of looking and seeing things is very deep. But he was just an ordinary person like any one of us. I don't know how or why he was able to look and see like that, but it is exactly the way we practice mindfulness. We try to be in touch with life and look deeply as we drink our tea, walk, sit down, or arrange flowers. The secret of the success is that you are really yourself, and when you are really yourself, you can encounter life in the present moment.

Breathing Room

We have a room for everything—eating, sleeping, watching TV—but we have no room for mindfulness. I recommend that we set up a small room in our homes and call it a "breathing room," where we can be alone and practice just breathing and smiling, at least in difficult moments. That little room should be regarded as an Embassy of the Kingdom of Peace. It should be respected, and not violated by anger, shouting, or things like that. When a child is about to be shouted at, she can take refuge in that room. Neither the father nor the mother can shout at her anymore. She is safe within the grounds of the Embassy. Parents sometimes will need to take refuge in that room, also, to sit down, breathe, smile, and restore themselves. Therefore, that room is for the benefit of the whole family.

I suggest that the breathing room be decorated very simply, and not be too bright. You may want to have a small bell, one with a beautiful sound, a few cushions or chairs, and perhaps a vase of flowers to remind us of our true nature. You or your children can arrange flowers in mindfulness, smiling. Every time you feel a little upset, you know that the best thing to do is to go to that room, open the door slowly, sit down, invite the bell to sound—in my country we don't say "strike" or "hit" a bell—and begin to breathe. The bell will help not only the person in the breathing room, but the others in the house as well.

Suppose your husband is irritated. Since he has learned the practice of breathing, he knows that the best thing is to go into that room, sit down, and practice. You may not realize where he has gone; you were busy cutting carrots in the kitchen. But you suffer also, because you and he just had some kind of altercation. You are cutting the carrots a bit strongly, because the energy of the anger is translated into the movement. Suddenly, you hear the bell, and you know what to do. You stop cutting and you breathe in and out. You feel better, and you may smile, thinking about your husband, who knows what to do when he gets angry. He is now sitting in the breathing room, breathing and smiling. That's wonderful; not many people do that. Suddenly, a feeling of tenderness arises, and you feel much better. After three breaths, you begin to cut the carrots again, but this time, quite differently.

Your child, who was witnessing the scene, knew that a kind of tempest was going to break. She withdrew to her room, closed the door, and silently waited. But instead of a storm, she heard the bell, and she understood what was going on. She feels so relieved, and she wants to show her appreciation to her father. She goes slowly to the breathing room, opens the door, and quietly enters and sits down beside him to show her support. That helps him very much. He already felt ready to go out—he is able to smile now—but since his daughter is sitting there, he wants to sound the bell again for his daughter to breathe.

In the kitchen, you hear the second bell and you know that cutting carrots may not be the best thing to do now. So, you put down your knife and go into the breathing room. Your husband is aware that the door is opening and you are coming in. So, although he is now all right, since you are coming, he stays on for some time longer and sounds the bell for you to breathe. This is a beautiful scene. If you are very wealthy, you can buy a precious painting by van Gogh and hang it in your living room. But it will be less beautiful than this scene in the breathing room. The practice of peace and reconciliation is one of the most vital and artistic of human actions.

I know of families where children go into a breathing room after breakfast, sit down, and breathe, "in-out-one," "in-out-two," "in-out-three," and so on up to ten, and then they go to school. If your child doesn't wish to breathe ten times, perhaps three times is enough. Beginning the day this way is very beautiful and very helpful to the whole family. If you are mindful in the morning and try to nourish mindfulness throughout the day, you may be able to come home at the end of a day with a smile, which proves that mindfulness is still there.

I believe that every home should have one room for breathing. Simple practices like conscious breathing and smiling are very important. They can change our civilization.

Continuing the Journey

We have walked together in mindfulness, learning how to breathe and smile in full awareness, at home, at work, and throughout the day. We have discussed eating mindfully, washing the dishes, driving, answering the telephone, and even cutting the grass with a scythe. Mindfulness is the foundation of a happy life.

But how can we deal with difficult emotions? What should we do when we feel anger, hatred, remorse, or sadness? There are many practices I have learned and a number I have discovered during the past forty years for working with these kinds of mental states. Shall we continue our journey together and try some of these practices?

PART TWO

Transformation and Healing

The River of Feelings

Our feelings play a very important part in directing all of our thoughts and actions. In us, there is a river of feelings, in which every drop of water is a different feeling, and each feeling relies on all the others for its existence. To observe it, we just sit on the bank of the river and identify each feeling as it surfaces, flows by, and disappears.

There are three sorts of feelings—pleasant, unpleasant, and neutral. When we have an unpleasant feeling, we may want to chase it away. But it is more effective to return to our conscious breathing and just observe it, identifying it silently to ourselves: "Breathing in, I know there is an unpleasant feeling in me. Breathing out, I know there is an unpleasant feeling in me." Calling a feeling by its name, such as "anger," "sorrow," "joy," or "happiness," helps us identify it clearly and recognize it more deeply.

We can use our breathing to be in contact with our feelings and accept them. If our breathing is light and calm—a natural result of conscious breathing—our mind and body will slowly become light, calm, and clear, and our feelings also. Mindful observation is based on the principle of "non-duality": our feeling is not separate from us or caused merely by something outside us; our feeling *is* us, and for the moment we *are* that feeling. We are neither drowned in nor terrorized by the feeling, nor do we reject it. Our attitude of not clinging to or rejecting our feelings is the attitude of letting go, an important part of meditation practice.

If we face our unpleasant feelings with care, affection, and nonviolence, we can transform them into the kind of energy that is healthy and has the capacity to nourish us. By the work of mindful observation, our unpleasant feelings can illuminate so much for us, offering us insight and understanding into ourselves and society.

Non-Surgery

Western medicine emphasizes surgery too much. Doctors want to take out the things that are not wanted. When we have something irregular in our body, too often they advise us to have an operation. The same seems to be true in psychotherapy. Therapists want to help us throw out what is unwanted and keep only what is wanted. But what is left may not be very much. If we try to throw away what we don't want, we may throw away most of ourselves.

Instead of acting as if we can dispose of parts of ourselves, we should learn the art of transformation. We can transform our anger, for example, into something more wholesome, like understanding. We do not need surgery to remove our anger. If we become angry at our anger, we will have two angers at the same time. We only have to observe it with love and attention. If we take care of our anger in this way, without trying to run away from it, it will transform itself. This is peacemaking. If we are peaceful in ourselves, we can make peace with our anger. We can deal with depression, anxiety, fear, or any unpleasant feeling in the same way.

Transforming Feelings

The first step in dealing with feelings is to recognize each feeling as it arises. The agent that does this is mindfulness. In the case of fear, for example, you bring out your mindfulness, look at your fear, and recognize it as fear. You know that fear springs from yourself and that mindfulness also springs from yourself. They are both in you, not fighting, but one taking care of the other.

The second step is to become one with the feeling. It is best not to say, "Go away, Fear. I don't like you. You are not me." It is much more effective to say, "Hello, Fear. How are you today?" Then you can invite the two aspects of yourself, mindfulness and fear, to shake hands as friends and become one. Doing this may seem frightening, but because you know that you are more than just your fear, you need not be afraid. As long as mindfulness is there, it can chaperone your fear. The fundamental practice is to nourish your mindfulness with conscious breathing, to keep it there, alive and strong. Although your mindfulness may not be very powerful in the beginning, if you nourish it, it will become stronger. As long as mindfulness is present, you will not drown in your fear. In fact, you begin transforming it the very moment you give birth to awareness in yourself.

The third step is to calm the feeling. As mindfulness is taking good care of your fear, you begin to calm it down. "Breathing in, I calm the activities of body and mind." You calm your feeling just by being with it, like a mother tenderly holding her crying baby. Feeling his mother's tenderness, the baby will calm down and stop crying. The mother is your mindfulness, born from the depth of your consciousness, and it will tend the feeling of pain. A mother holding her baby is one with her baby. If the mother is thinking of other things, the baby will not calm down. The mother has to put aside other things and just hold her baby. So, don't avoid your feeling. Don't say, "You are not important. You are only a feeling." Come and be one with it. You can say, "Breathing out, I calm my fear."

The fourth step is to release the feeling, to let it go. Because of your calm, you feel at ease, even in the midst of fear, and you know that your fear will not grow into something that will overwhelm you. When you know that you are capable of taking care of your fear, it is already reduced to the minimum, becoming softer and not so unpleasant. Now you can smile at it and let it go, but please do not stop yet. Calming and releasing are just medicines for the symptoms. You now have an opportunity to go deeper and work on transforming the source of your fear.

The fifth step is to look deeply. You look deeply into your baby—your feeling of fear—to see what is wrong, even after the baby has already stopped crying, after the fear is gone. You cannot hold your baby all the time, and therefore you have to look into him to see the cause of what is wrong. By looking, you will see what will help you begin to transform the feeling. You will realize, for example, that his suffering has many causes, inside and outside of his body. If something is wrong around him, if you put that in order, bringing tenderness and care to the situation, he will feel better. Looking into your baby, you see the elements that are causing him to cry, and when you see them, you will know what to do and what not to do to transform the feeling and be free.

This is a process similar to psychotherapy. Together with the patient, a therapist looks at the nature of the pain. Often, the therapist can uncover causes of suffering that stem from the way the patient looks at things, the beliefs he holds about himself, his culture, and the world. The therapist examines these viewpoints and beliefs with the patient, and together they help free him from the kind of prison he has been in. But the patient's efforts are crucial. A teacher has to give birth to the teacher within his student, and a psychotherapist has to give birth to the psycho-therapist within his patient. The patient's "internal psychother-apist" can then work full-time in a very effective way.

The therapist does not treat the patient by simply giving him another set of beliefs. She tries to help him see which kinds of ideas and beliefs have led to his suffering. Many patients want to get rid of their painful feelings, but they do not want to get rid of their beliefs, the viewpoints that are the very roots of their feel-ings. So therapist and patient have to work together to help the patient see things as they are. The same is true when we use mindfulness to transform our feelings. After recognizing the feeling, becoming one with it, calming it down, and releasing it, we can look deeply into its causes, which are often based on in-accurate perceptions. As soon as we understand the causes and nature of our feelings, they begin to transform themselves.

Mindfulness of Anger

Anger is an unpleasant feeling. It is like a blazing flame that burns up our self-control and causes us to say and do things that we regret later. When someone is angry, we can see clearly that he or she is abiding in hell. Anger and hatred are the materials from which hell is made. A mind without anger is cool, fresh, and sane. The absence of anger is the basis of real happiness, the basis of love and compassion.

When our anger is placed under the lamp of mindfulness, it immediately begins to lose some of its destructive nature. We can say to ourselves, "Breathing in, I know that anger is in me. Breathing out, I know that I am my anger." If we follow our breathing closely while we identify and mindfully observe our anger, it can no longer monopolize our consciousness.

Awareness can be called upon to be a companion for our anger. Our awareness of our anger does not suppress it or drive it out. It just looks after it. This is a very important principle. Mindfulness is not a judge. It is more like an older sister looking after and comforting her younger sister in an affectionate and caring way. We can concentrate on our breathing in order to maintain this mindfulness and know ourselves fully.

When we are angry, we are not usually inclined to return to ourselves. We want to think about the person who is making us angry, to think about his hateful aspects—his rudeness, dishonesty, cruelty, maliciousness, and so on. The more we think about him, listen to him, or look at him, the more our anger flares. His dishonesty and hatefulness may be real, imaginary, or exaggerated, but, in fact, the root of the problem is the anger itself, and we have to come back and look first of all inside ourselves. It is best if we do not listen to or look at the person whom we consider to be the cause of our anger. Like a fireman, we have to pour water on the blaze first and not waste time looking for the one who set the house on fire. "Breathing in, I know that I am angry. Breathing out, I know that I must put all my energy into caring for my anger." So we avoid thinking about the other person, and we refrain from doing or saying anything as long as our anger persists. If we put all our mind into observing our anger, we will avoid doing any damage that we may regret later.

When we are angry, our anger is our very self. To suppress or chase it away is to suppress or chase away our self. When we are joyful, we are the joy. When we are angry, we are the anger. When anger is born in us, we can be aware that anger is an energy in us, and we can accept that energy in order to transform it into another kind of energy. When we have a compost bin filled with organic material which is decomposing and smelly, we know that we can transform the waste into beautiful flowers. At first, we may see the compost and the flowers as opposite, but when we look deeply, we see that the flowers already exist in the compost, and the compost already exists in the flowers. It only takes a couple of weeks for a flower to decompose. When a good organic gardener looks into her compost, she can see that, and she does not feel sad or disgusted. Instead, she values the rotting material and does not discriminate against it. It takes only a few months for compost to give birth to flowers. We need the insight and non-dual vision of the organic gardener with regard to our anger. We need not be afraid of it or reject it. We know that anger can be a kind of compost, and that it is within its power to give birth to something beautiful. We need anger in the way the organic gardener needs compost. If we know how to accept our anger, we already have some peace and joy. Gradually we can transform anger completely into peace, love, and understanding.

Pillow-Pounding

Expressing anger is not always the best way to deal with it. In expressing anger we might be practicing or rehearsing it, and making it stronger in the depth of our consciousness. Expressing anger to the person we are angry at can cause a lot of damage.

Some of us may prefer to go into our room, lock the door, and punch a pillow. We call this "getting in touch with our anger." But I don't think this is getting in touch with our anger at all. In fact, I don't think it is even getting in touch with our pillow. If we are really in touch with the pillow, we know what a pillow is and we won't hit it. Still, this technique may work temporarily because while pounding the pillow, we expend a lot of energy, and after a while, we are exhausted and we feel better. But the roots of our anger are still intact, and if we go out and eat some nourishing food, our energy will be renewed. If the seeds of our anger are watered again, our anger will be reborn, and we will have to pound the pillow again.

Pillow-pounding may provide some relief, but it is not very long-lasting. In order to have real transformation, we have to deal with the roots of our anger—looking deeply into its causes. If we don't, the seeds of anger will grow again. If we practice mindful living, planting new, healthy, wholesome seeds, they will take care of our anger, and they may transform it without our asking them to do so.

Our mindfulness will take care of everything, as the sunshine takes care of the vegetation. The sunshine does not seem to do much, it just shines on the vegetation, but it transforms everything. Poppies close up every time it gets dark, but when the sun shines on them for one or two hours, they open. The sun penetrates into the flowers, and at some point, the flowers cannot resist, they just have to open up. In the same way, mindfulness, if practiced continuously, will provide a kind of transformation within the flower of our anger, and it will open and show us its own nature. When we understand the nature, the roots, of our anger, we will be freed from it.

Walking Meditation When Angry

When anger arises, we may wish to go outside to practice walking meditation. The fresh air, the green trees, and the plants will help us greatly. We can practice like this:

Breathing in, I know that anger is here.
Breathing out, I know that the anger is me.
Breathing in, I know that anger is unpleasant.
Breathing out, I know this feeling will pass.
Breathing in, I am calm.
Breathing out, I am strong enough to take care of this anger.

To lessen the unpleasant feeling brought about by the anger, we give our whole heart and mind to the practice of walking meditation, combining our breath with our steps and giving full attention to the contact between the soles of our feet and the earth. As we walk, we recite this verse, and wait until we are calm enough to look directly at the anger. Until then, we can enjoy our breathing, our walking, and the beauties of our environment. After a while, our anger will subside and we will feel stronger. Then we can begin to observe the anger directly and try to understand it.

Cooking Our Potatoes

Thanks to the illuminating light of awareness, after practicing mindful observation for a while, we begin to see the primary causes of our anger. Meditation helps us look deeply into things in order to see their nature. If we look into our anger, we can see its roots, such as misunderstanding, clumsiness, injustice, resentment, or conditioning. These roots can be present in ourselves and in the person who played the principal role in precipitating our anger. We observe mindfully in order to be able to see and to understand. Seeing and understanding are the elements of liberation that bring about love and compassion. The method of mindful observation in order to see and understand the roots of the anger is a method that has lasting effectiveness.

We cannot eat raw potatoes, but we don't throw them away just because they are raw. We know we can cook them. So, we put them into a pot of water, put a lid on, and put the pot on the fire. The fire is mindfulness, the practice of breathing consciously and focusing on our anger. The lid symbolizes our concentration, because it prevents the heat from going out of the pot. When we are practicing breathing in and out, looking into our anger, we need some concentration in order for our practice to be strong. Therefore, we turn away from all distractions and focus on the problem. If we go out into nature, among the trees and flowers, the practice is easier.

As soon as we put the pot on the fire, a change occurs. The water begins to warm up. Ten minutes later, it boils, but we have to keep the fire going a while longer in order to cook our potatoes. As we practice being aware of our breathing and our anger, a transformation is already occurring. After half an hour, we lift the lid and smell something different. We know that we can eat our potatoes now. Anger has been transformed into another kind of energy—understanding and compassion.

The Roots of Anger

Anger is rooted in our lack of understanding of ourselves and of the causes, deep-seated as well as immediate, that brought about this unpleasant state of affairs. Anger is also rooted in desire, pride, agitation, and suspicion. The primary roots of our anger are in ourselves. Our environment and other people are only secondary. It is not difficult for us to accept the enormous damage brought about by a natural disaster, such as an earthquake or a flood. But when damage is caused by another person, we don't have much patience. We know that earthquakes and floods have causes, and we should see that the person who has precipitated our anger also has reasons, deep-seated and immediate, for what he has done.

For instance, someone who speaks badly to us may have been spoken to in exactly the same way just the day before, or by his alcoholic father when he was a child. When we see and understand these kinds of causes, we can begin to be free from our anger. I am not saying that someone who viciously attacks us should not be disciplined. But what is most important is that we first take care of the seeds of negativity in ourselves. Then if someone needs to be helped or disciplined, we will do so out of compassion, not anger and retribution. If we genuinely try to understand the suffering of another person, we are more likely to act in a way that will help him overcome his suffering and confusion, and that will help all of us.

Internal Formations

There is a term in Buddhist psychology that can be translated as "internal formations," "fetters," or "knots." When we have a sensory input, depending on how we receive it, a knot may be tied in us. When someone speaks unkindly to us, if we understand the reason and do not take his or her words to heart, we will not feel irritated at all, and no knot will be tied. But if we do not understand why we were spoken to that way and we become irritated, a knot will be tied in us. The absence of clear understanding is the basis for every knot.

If we practice full awareness, we will be able to recognize internal formations as soon as they are formed, and we will find ways to transform them. For example, a wife may hear her husband boasting at a party, and inside herself she feels the formation of a lack of respect. If she discusses this with her husband, they may come to a clear understanding, and the knot in her will be untied easily. Internal formations need our full attention as soon as they manifest, while they are still weak, so that the work of transformation is easy.

If we do not untie our knots when they form, they will grow tighter and stronger. Our conscious, reasoning mind knows that negative feelings such as anger, fear, and regret are not wholly acceptable to ourselves or society, so it finds ways to repress them, to push them into remote areas of our consciousness in order to forget them. Because we want to avoid suffering, we create defense mechanisms that deny the existence of these negative feelings and give us the impression we have peace within ourselves. But our internal formations are always looking for ways to manifest as destructive images, feelings, thoughts, words, or behavior.

The way to deal with unconscious internal formations is, first of all, to find ways to become aware of them. By practicing mindful breathing, we may gain access to some of the knots that are tied inside us. When we are aware of our images, feelings, thoughts, words, and behavior, we can ask ourselves questions such as: Why did I feel uncomfortable when I heard him say that? Why did I say that to him? Why do I always think of my mother when I see that woman? Why didn't I like that character in the movie? Whom did I hate in the past whom she resembles? Observing closely like this can gradually bring the internal formations that are buried in us into the realm of the conscious mind.

During sitting meditation, after we have closed the doors and windows of sensory input, the internal formations buried inside us sometimes reveal themselves as images, feelings, or thoughts. We may notice a feeling of anxiety, fear, or unpleasantness whose cause we cannot understand. So we shine the light of our mindfulness on it, and prepare ourselves to see this image, feeling, or thought, in all its complexity. When it begins to show its face, it may gather strength and become more intense. We may find it so strong that it robs us of our peace, joy, and ease, and we may not want to be in contact with it anymore. We may want to move our attention to another object of meditation or discontinue the meditation altogether; we may feel sleepy or say that we prefer to meditate some other time. In psychology, this is called resistance. We are afraid to bring into our conscious mind the feelings of pain that are buried in us, because they will make us suffer. But if we have been practicing breathing and smiling for some time, we will have developed the capacity to sit still and just observe our fears. As we keep in contact with our breathing and continue to smile, we can say, "Hello, Fear. There you are again."

There are people who practice sitting meditation many hours a day and never really face their feelings. Some of them say that feelings are not important, and they prefer to give their attention to metaphysical subjects. I am not suggesting that these other subjects of meditation are unimportant, but if they are not considered in relation to our real problems, our meditation is not really very valuable or helpful.

If we know how to live every moment in an awakened way, we will be aware of what is going on in our feelings and perceptions in the present moment, and we will not let knots form or become tighter in our consciousness. And if we know how to observe our feelings, we can find the roots of long-standing internal formations and transform them, even those that have become quite strong.

Living Together

When we live with another person, to protect each other's happiness, we should help one another transform the internal formations that we produce together. By practicing understanding and loving speech, we can help each other a great deal. Happiness is no longer an individual matter. If the other person is not happy, we will not be happy either. To transform the other person's knots will help bring about our own happiness as well. A wife can create internal formations in her husband, and a husband can do so in his wife, and if they continue to create knots in each other, one day there will be no happiness left. Therefore, as soon as a knot is created, the wife, for example, should know that a knot has just been tied in her. She should not overlook it. She should take the time to observe it and, with her husband's help, transform it. She might say, "Darling, I think we'd better discuss a conflict I see growing." This is easy when the states of mind of husband and wife are still light and not filled with too many knots.

The root cause of any internal formation is a lack of understanding. If we can see the misunderstanding that was present during the creation of a knot, we can easily untie it. To practice mindful observation is to look deeply to be able to see the nature and causes of something. One important benefit of this kind of insight is the untying of our knots.

Suchness

In Buddhism, the word "suchness" is used to mean "the essence or particular characteristics of a thing or a person, its true nature." Each person has his or her suchness. If we want to live in peace and happiness with a person, we have to see the suchness of that person. Once we see it, we understand him or her, and there will be no trouble. We can live peacefully and happily together.

When we bring natural gas into our homes for heating and cooking, we know the suchness of gas. We know that gas is dangerous—it can kill us if we are not mindful. But we also know that we need the gas in order to cook, so we do not hesitate to bring it into our homes. The same is true of electricity. We could get electrocuted by it, but when we are mindful, it can help us, and there is no problem, because we know something about the suchness of electricity. A person is the same. If we do not know enough about the suchness of that person, we may get ourselves into trouble. But if we know, then we can enjoy each other very much and benefit a lot from one another. The key is knowing a person's suchness. We do not expect a person always to be a flower. We have to understand his or her garbage as well.

Look into Your Hand

I have a friend who is an artist. Before he left Vietnam forty years ago, his mother held his hand and told him, "Whenever you miss me, look into your hand, and you will see me immediately." How penetrating these simple, sincere words!

Over the years, my friend looked into his hand many times.

The presence of his mother is not just genetic. Her spirit, her hopes, and her life are also in him. When he looks into his hand, he can see thousands of generations before him and thousands of generations after him. He can see that he exists not only in the evolutionary tree branching along the axis of time, but also in the network of interdependent relations. He told me that he never feels lonely.

When my niece came to visit me last summer, I offered her "Look into Your Hand" as a subject for her meditation. I told her that every pebble, every leaf, and every butterfly are present in her hand.

Parents

When I think of my mother, I cannot separate her image from my idea of love, for love was the natural ingredient in the sweet, soft tones of her voice. On the day I lost my mother, I wrote in my diary, "The greatest tragedy in my life has just happened." Even as an adult living away from my mother, her loss left me feeling as abandoned as a small orphan.

I know that many friends in the West do not feel the same way about their parents. I have heard many stories about parents who have hurt their children so much, planting many seeds of suffering in them. But I believe that the parents did not mean to plant those seeds. They did not intend to make their children suffer. Maybe they received the same kind of seeds from their parents. There is a continuation in the transmission of seeds, and their father and mother might have gotten those seeds from their grandfather and grandmother. Most of us are victims of a kind of living that is not mindful, and the practice of mindful living, of meditation, can stop these kinds of suffering and end the transmission of such sorrow to our children and grandchildren. We can break the cycle by not allowing these kinds of seeds of suffering to be transmitted to our children, our friends, or anyone else.

A fourteen-year-old boy who practices at Plum Village told me this story. When he was eleven, he was very angry at his father. Every time he fell down and hurt himself, his father would shout at him. The boy vowed to himself that when he grew up, he would be different. But last year, his little sister was playing with other children and she fell off a swing and scraped her knee. It was bleeding, and the boy became very angry. He wanted to shout at her, "How stupid! Why did you do that?" But he caught himself. Because he had practiced breathing and mindfulness, he could recognize his anger and he did not act on it.

The adults were taking good care of his sister, washing her wound and putting a band-aid on it, so he walked away slowly and practiced breathing on his anger. Suddenly he saw that he was exactly like his father. He told me, "I realized that if I didn't do something about the anger in me, I would transmit it to my children." At the same time, he saw something else. He saw that his father may have been a victim just like him. The seeds of his father's anger might have been transmitted by his grandparents. It was a remarkable insight for a fourteen-year-old boy, but because he had been practicing mindfulness, he could see like that. "I told myself to continue practicing in order to transform my anger into something else." And after a few months, his anger disappeared. Then he was able to bring the fruit of his practice back to his father, and he told him that he used to be angry at him, but now he understood. He said he wished that his father would practice also, in order to transform his own seeds of anger. We usually think that parents have to nourish their children, but sometimes the children can bring enlightenment to the parents and help transform them.

When we look at our parents with compassion, often we see that our parents are only victims who never had the chance to practice mindfulness. They could not transform the suffering in themselves. But if we see them with compassionate eyes, we can offer them joy, peace, and forgiveness. In fact, when we look deeply, we discover that it is impossible to drop all identity with our parents.

Whenever we take a bath or a shower, if we look closely at our body, we will see that it is a gift from our parents and their parents. As we wash each part of our body, we can meditate on the nature of the body and the nature of life, asking ourselves, "To whom does this body belong? Who has given this body to me? What has been given?" If we meditate in this way, we will discover that there are three components: the giver, the gift, and the one who receives the gift. The giver is our parents; we are the continuation of our parents and our ancestors. The gift is our body itself. The one who receives the gift is us. As we continue to meditate on this, we see clearly that the giver, the gift, and the receiver are one. All three are present in our body. When we are deeply in touch with the present moment, we can see that all our ancestors and all future generations are present in us. Seeing this, we will know what to do and what not to do—for ourselves, our ancestors, our children, and their children.

Nourishing Healthy Seeds

Consciousness exists on two levels: as seeds and as manifestations of these seeds. Suppose we have a seed of anger in us. When conditions are favorable, that seed may manifest as a zone of energy called anger. It is burning, and it makes us suffer a lot. It is very difficult for us to be joyful at the moment the seed of anger manifests.

Every time a seed has an occasion to manifest itself, it produces new seeds of the same kind. If we are angry for five minutes, new seeds of anger are produced and deposited in the soil of our unconscious mind during those five minutes. That is why we have to be careful in selecting the kind of life we lead and the emotions we express. When I smile, the seeds of smiling and joy have come up. As long as they manifest, new seeds of smiling and joy are planted. But if I don't practice smiling for a number of years, that seed will weaken, and I may not be able to smile anymore.

There are many kinds of seeds in us, both good and bad. Some were planted during our lifetime, and some were transmitted by our parents, our ancestors, and our society. In a tiny grain of corn, there is the knowledge, transmitted by previous generations, of how to sprout and how to make leaves, flowers, and ears of corn. Our body and our mind also have knowledge that has been transmitted by previous generations. Our ancestors and our parents have given us seeds of joy, peace, and happiness, as well as seeds of sorrow, anger, and so on.

Every time we practice mindful living, we plant healthy seeds and strengthen the healthy seeds already in us. Healthy seeds function similarly to antibodies. When a virus enters our bloodstream, our body reacts and antibodies come and surround it, take care of it, and transform it. This is true with our psychological seeds as well. If we plant wholesome, healing, refreshing seeds, they will take care of the negative seeds, even without our asking them. To succeed, we need to cultivate a good reserve of refreshing seeds.

One day, in the village where I live, we lost a very close friend, a Frenchman who helped us considerably in setting up Plum

Village. He had a heart attack and died during the night. In the morning we learned of his passing. He was such a gracious person, and he gave us a lot of joy every time we spent a few minutes with him. We felt that he was joy and peace itself. The morning we found out about his death, we regretted very much that we had not spent more time with him.

That night, I couldn't sleep. The loss of a friend like him was so painful. But I had to deliver a lecture the next morning, and I wanted to sleep, so I practiced breathing. It was a cold, winter night, and I was lying in bed visualizing the beautiful trees in the yard of my hermitage. Years before, I had planted three beautiful cedars, a variety from the Himalayas. The trees are now very big, and, during walking meditation, I used to stop and hug these beautiful cedars, breathing in and out. The cedars always responded to my hugging, I am sure of it. So I lay in bed, and just breathed in and out, becoming the cedars and my breath. I felt much better, but still I couldn't sleep. Finally I invited into my consciousness the image of a delightful Vietnamese child named Little Bamboo. She came to Plum Village when she was two years old, and she was so cute that everyone wanted to hold her in their arms, especially the children. They didn't let Little Bamboo walk on the ground! Now she is six years old, and holding her in your arms, you feel very fresh, very wonderful. So I invited her to come up into my consciousness, and I practiced breathing and smiling on her image. In just a few moments, I fell soundly asleep.

Each of us needs a reserve of seeds that are beautiful, healthy, and strong enough to help us during difficult moments. Sometimes, because the block of pain in us is so big, even though a flower is right in front of us, we cannot touch it. At that moment, we know that we need help. If we have a strong storehouse of healthy seeds, we can invite several of them to come up and help us. If you have a friend who is very close to you, who understands you, if you know that when you sit close to her, even without saying anything, you will feel better, then you can invite her image up into your consciousness, and the "two" of you can "breathe together." Doing just this may be a big help in difficult moments.

But if you have not seen your friend in a long time, her image may be too weak in your consciousness to come easily to you. If you know that she is the only person who can help you re-establish your balance and if your image of her is already too weak, there is only one thing to do: buy a ticket and go to her, so that she is with you not as a seed, but as a real person.

If you go to her, you have to know how to spend the time well, because your time with her is limited. When you arrive, sit close to her, and right away you will feel stronger. But you know that soon you will have to return home, so you have to take the opportunity to practice full awareness in each precious moment while you are there. Your friend can help you re-establish the balance within you, but that is not enough. You yourself must become strong inside, in order to feel all right when you are alone again. That is why, sitting with her or walking with her, you need to practice mindfulness. If you don't, if you just use her presence to ameliorate your suffering, the seed of her image will not become strong enough to sustain you when you return home. We need to practice mindfulness all the time so that we plant healing, refreshing seeds in ourselves. Then, when we need them, they will take care of us.

What's Not Wrong?

We often ask, "What's wrong?" Doing so, we invite painful seeds of sorrow to come up and manifest. We feel suffering, anger, and depression, and produce more such seeds. We would be much happier if we tried to stay in touch with the healthy, joyful seeds inside of us and around us. We should learn to ask, "What's not wrong?" and be in touch with that. There are so many elements in the world and within our bodies, feelings, perceptions, and consciousness that are wholesome, refreshing, and healing. If we block ourselves, if we stay in the prison of our sorrow, we will not be in touch with these healing elements.

Life is filled with many wonders, like the blue sky, the sunshine, the eyes of a baby. Our breathing, for example, can be very enjoyable. I enjoy breathing every day. But many people appreciate the joy of breathing only when they have asthma or a stuffed-up nose. We don't need to wait until we have asthma to enjoy our breathing. Awareness of the precious elements of happiness is itself the practice of right mindfulness. Elements like these are within us and all around us. In each second of our lives we can enjoy them. If we do so, seeds of peace, joy, and happiness will be planted in us, and they will become strong. The secret to happiness is happiness itself. Wherever we are, any time, we have the capacity to enjoy the sunshine, the presence of each other, the wonder of our breathing. We don't have to travel anywhere else to do so. We can be in touch with these things right now.

Blaming Never Helps

When you plant lettuce, if it does not grow well, you don't blame the lettuce. You look into the reasons it is not doing well. It may need fertilizer, or more water, or less sun. You never blame the lettuce. Yet if we have problems with our friends or our family, we blame the other person. But if we know how to take care of them, they will grow well, like lettuce. Blaming has no positive effect at all, nor does trying to persuade using reason and arguments. That is my experience. No blame, no reasoning, no argument, just understanding. If you understand, and you show that you understand, you can love, and the situation will change.

One day in Paris, I gave a lecture about not blaming the lettuce. After the talk, I was doing walking meditation by myself, and when I turned the corner of a building, I overheard an eight-year-old girl telling her mother, "Mommy, remember to water me. I am your lettuce." I was so pleased that she had understood my point completely. Then I heard her mother reply, "Yes, my daughter, and I am your lettuce also. So please don't forget to water me too." Mother and daughter practicing together, it was very beautiful.

Understanding

Understanding and love are not two things, but just one. Suppose your son wakes up one morning and sees that it is already quite late. He decides to wake up his younger sister, to give her enough time to eat breakfast before going to school. It happens that she is grouchy and instead of saying, "Thank you for waking me up," she says, "Shut up! Leave me alone!" and kicks him. He will probably get angry, thinking, "I woke her up nicely. Why did she kick me?" He may want to go to the kitchen and tell you about it, or even kick her back.

But then he remembers that during the night his sister coughed a lot, and he realizes that she must be sick. Maybe she behaved so meanly because she has a cold. At that moment, he understands, and he is not angry at all anymore. When you understand, you cannot help but love. You cannot get angry. To develop understanding, you have to practice looking at all living beings with the eyes of compassion. When you understand, you cannot help but love. And when you love, you naturally act in a way that can relieve the suffering of people.

Real Love

We really have to understand the person we want to love. If our love is only a will to possess, it is not love. If we only think of ourselves, if we know only our own needs and ignore the needs of the other person, we cannot love. We must look deeply in order to see and understand the needs, aspirations, and suffering of the person we love. This is the ground of real love. You cannot resist loving another person when you really understand him or her.

From time to time, sit close to the one you love, hold his or her hand, and ask, "Darling, do I understand you enough? Or am I making you suffer? Please tell me so that I can learn to love you properly. I don't want to make you suffer, and if I do so because of my ignorance, please tell me so that I can love you better, so that you can be happy." If you say this in a voice that communicates your real openness to understand, the other person may cry.

That is a good sign, because it means the door of understanding is opening and everything will be possible again.

Maybe a father does not have time or is not brave enough to ask his son such a question. Then the love between them will not be as full as it could be. We need courage to ask these questions, but if we don't ask, the more we love, the more we may destroy the people we are trying to love. True love needs understanding. With understanding, the one we love will certainly flower.

Meditation on Compassion

Love is a mind that brings peace, joy, and happiness to another person. Compassion is a mind that removes the suffering that is present in the other. We all have the seeds of love and compassion in our minds, and we can develop these fine and wonderful sources of energy. We can nurture the unconditional love that does not expect anything in return and therefore does not lead to anxiety and sorrow.

The essence of love and compassion is understanding, the ability to recognize the physical, material, and psychological suffering of others, to put ourselves "inside the skin" of the other. We "go inside" their body, feelings, and mental formations, and witness for ourselves their suffering. Shallow observation as an outsider is not enough to see their suffering. We must become one with the object of our observation. When we are in contact with another's suffering, a feeling of compassion is born in us. Compassion means, literally, "to suffer with."

We begin by choosing as the object of our meditation someone who is undergoing physical or material suffering, someone who is weak and easily ill, poor or oppressed, or has no protection. This kind of suffering is easy for us to see. After that, we can practice being in contact with more subtle forms of suffering. Sometimes the other person does not seem to be suffering at all, but we may notice that he has sorrows which have left their marks in hidden ways. People with more than enough material comforts also suffer. We look deeply at the person who is the object of our meditation on compassion, both during sitting meditation and when we are actually in contact with him. We must allow enough time to be really in deep contact with his suffering. We continue to observe him until compassion arises and penetrates our being.

When we observe deeply in this way, the fruit of our meditation will naturally transform into some kind of action. We will not just say, "I love him very much," but instead, "I will do something so that he will suffer less." The mind of compassion is truly present when it is effective in removing another person's suffering. We have to find ways to nourish and express our compassion. When we come into contact with the other person, our thoughts and actions should express our mind of compassion, even if that person says and does things that are not easy to accept. We practice in this way until we see clearly that our love is not contingent upon the other person being lovable. Then we can know that our mind of compassion is firm and authentic. We ourselves will be more at ease, and the person who has been the object of our meditation will also benefit eventually. His suffering will slowly diminish, and his life will gradually be brighter and more joyful as a result of our compassion.

We can also meditate on the suffering of those who cause us to suffer. Anyone who has made us suffer is undoubtedly suffering too. We only need to follow our breathing and look deeply, and naturally we will see his suffering. A part of his difficulties and sorrows may have been brought about by his parents' lack of skill when he was still young. But his parents themselves may have been victims of their parents; the suffering has been transmitted from generation to generation and been reborn in him. If we see that, we will no longer blame him for making us suffer, because we know that he is also a victim. To look deeply is to understand. Once we understand the reasons he has acted badly, our bitterness towards him will vanish, and we will long for him to suffer less. We will feel cool and light, and we can smile. We do not need the other person to be present in order to bring about reconciliation. When we look deeply, we become reconciled with ourselves, and, for us, the problem no longer exists. Sooner or later, he will see our attitude and will share in the freshness of the stream of love which is flowing naturally from our heart.

Meditation on Love

The mind of love brings peace, joy, and happiness to ourselves and others. Mindful observation is the element which nourishes the tree of understanding, and compassion and love are the most beautiful flowers. When we realize the mind of love, we have to go to the one who has been the object of our mindful observation, so that our mind of love is not just an object of our imagination, but a source of energy which has a real effect in the world.

The meditation on love is not just sitting still and visualizing that our love will spread out into space like waves of sound or light. Sound and light have the ability to penetrate everywhere, and love and compassion can do the same. But if our love is only a kind of imagination, then it is not likely to have any real effect. It is in the midst of our daily life and in our actual contact with others that we can know whether our mind of love is really present and how stable it is. If love is real, it will be evident in our daily life, in the way we relate with people and the world.

The source of love is deep in us, and we can help others realize a lot of happiness. One word, one action, or one thought can reduce another person's suffering and bring him joy. One word can give comfort and confidence, destroy doubt, help someone avoid a mistake, reconcile a conflict, or open the door to liberation. One action can save a person's life or help him take advantage of a rare opportunity. One thought can do the same, because thoughts always lead to words and actions. If love is in our heart, every thought, word, and deed can bring about a miracle. Because understanding is the very foundation of love, words and actions that emerge from our love are always helpful.

Hugging Meditation

Hugging is a beautiful Western custom, and we from the East would like to contribute the practice of conscious breathing to it. When you hold a child in your arms, or hug your mother, or your husband, or your friend, if you breathe in and out three times, your happiness will be multiplied at least tenfold.

If you are distracted, thinking about other things, your hug will be distracted also, not very deep, and you may not enjoy hugging very much. So when you hug your child, your friend, your spouse, I recommend that you first breathe in and out consciously and return to the present moment. Then, while you hold him or her in your arms, breathe three times consciously, and you will enjoy your hugging more than ever before.

We practiced hugging meditation at a retreat for psychotherapists in Colorado, and one retreatant, when he returned home to Philadelphia, hugged his wife at the airport in a way he had never hugged her before. Because of that, his wife attended our next retreat, in Chicago.

It takes time to become comfortable hugging this way. If you feel a little hollow inside, you may want to slap your friend's back while you hug him in order to prove that you are really there. But to be really there, you only need to breathe, and suddenly he becomes completely real. The two of you really exist in that moment. It may be one of the best moments in your life.

Suppose your daughter comes and presents herself to you. If you are not really there—if you are thinking of the past, worrying about the future, or possessed by anger or fear—the child, although standing in front of you, will not exist for you. She is like a ghost, and you may be like a ghost also. If you want to be with her, you have to return to the present moment. Breathing consciously, uniting body and mind, you make yourself into a real person again. When you become a real person, your daughter becomes real also. She is a wondrous presence, and a real encounter with life is possible at that moment. If you hold her in your arms and breathe, you will awaken to the preciousness of your loved one, and life is.

Investing in Friends

Even if we have a lot of money in the bank, we can die very easily from our suffering. So, investing in a friend, making a friend into a real friend, building a community of friends, is a much better source of security. We will have someone to lean on, to come to, during our difficult moments.

We can get in touch with the refreshing, healing elements within and around us thanks to the loving support of other people. If we have a good community of friends, we are very fortunate. To create a good community, we first have to transform ourselves into a good element of the community. After that, we can go to another person and help him or her become an element of the community. We build our network of friends that way. We have to think of friends and community as investments, as our most important asset. They can comfort us and help us in difficult times, and they can share our joy and happiness.

It Is a Great Joy
to Hold Your Grandchild

You know that elderly people are very sad when they have to live separately from their children and grandchildren. This is one of the things in the West that I do not like. In my country, aged people have the right to live with the younger people. It is the grandparents who tell fairy tales to the children. When they get old, their skin is cold and wrinkled, and it is a great joy for them to hold their grandchild, so warm and tender. When a person grows old, his deepest hope is to have a grandchild to hold in his arms. He hopes for it day and night, and when he hears that his daughter or daughter-in-law is pregnant, he is so happy. Nowadays the elderly have to go to a home where they live only among other aged people. Just once a week they receive a short visit, and afterwards they feel even sadder. We have to find ways for old and young people to live together again. It will make all of us very happy.

Community
of Mindful Living

The foundation of a good community is a daily life that is joyful and happy. In Plum Village, children are the center of attention. Each adult is responsible for helping the children be happy, because we know that if the children are happy, it is easy for the adults to be happy.

When I was a child, families were bigger. Parents, cousins, uncles, aunts, grandparents, and children all lived together. The houses were surrounded by trees where we could hang hammocks and organize picnics. In those times, people did not have many of the problems we have today. Now our families are very small, just mother, father, and one or two children. When the parents have a problem, the whole family feels the effects. Even if the children go into the bathroom to try to get away, they can feel the heavy atmosphere. They may grow up with seeds of suffering and never be truly happy. Formerly, when mom and dad had problems, the children could escape by going to an aunt or uncle, or other family member. They still had someone to look up to, and the atmosphere was not so threatening.

I think that communities of mindful living, where we can visit a network of "aunts, uncles, and cousins," may help us replace our former big families. Each of us needs to "belong to" such a place, where each feature of the landscape, the sounds of the bell, and even the buildings are designed to remind us to return to awareness. I imagine that there will be beautiful practice centers where regular retreats will be organized, and individuals and families will go there to learn and practice the art of mindful living.

The people who live there should emanate peace and freshness, the fruits of living in awareness. They will be like beautiful trees, and the visitors will want to come and sit under their shade. Even when they cannot actually visit, they only need to think of it and smile, and they will feel themselves becoming peaceful and happy.

We can also transform our own family or household into a community that practices harmony and awareness. Together we can practice breathing and smiling, sitting together, drinking tea together in mindfulness. If we have a bell, the bell is also part of the community, because the bell helps us practice. If we have a meditation cushion, the cushion is also part of the community, as are many other things that help us practice mindfulness, such as the air for breathing. If we live near a park or a riverbank, we can enjoy walking meditation there. All these efforts can help us establish a community at home. From time to time we can invite a friend to join us. Practicing mindfulness is much easier with a community.

Mindfulness Must Be Engaged

When I was in Vietnam, so many of our villages were being bombed. Along with my monastic brothers and sisters, I had to decide what to do. Should we continue to practice in our monasteries, or should we leave the meditation halls in order to help the people who were suffering under the bombs? After careful reflection, we decided to do both—to go out and help people and to do so in mindfulness. We called it engaged Buddhism. Mindfulness must be engaged. Once there is seeing, there must be acting. Otherwise, what is the use of seeing?

We must be aware of the real problems of the world. Then, with mindfulness, we will know what to do and what not to do to be of help. If we maintain awareness of our breathing and continue to practice smiling, even in difficult situations, many people, animals, and plants will benefit from our way of doing things. Are you massaging our Mother Earth every time your foot touches her? Are you planting seeds of joy and peace? I try to do exactly that with every step, and I know that our Mother Earth is most appreciative. Peace is every step. Shall we continue our journey?

PART THREE

Peace Is Every Step

Interbeing

If you are a poet, you will see clearly that there is a cloud floating in this sheet of paper. Without a cloud, there will be no rain; without rain, the trees cannot grow; and without trees, we cannot make paper. The cloud is essential for the paper to exist. If the cloud is not here, the sheet of paper cannot be here either. So we can say that the cloud and the paper *inter-are*. "Interbeing" is a word that is not in the dictionary yet, but if we combine the prefix "inter-" with the verb "to be," we have a new verb, inter-be.

If we look into this sheet of paper even more deeply, we can see the sunshine in it. Without sunshine, the forest cannot grow. In fact, nothing can grow without sunshine. And so, we know that the sunshine is also in this sheet of paper. The paper and the sunshine inter-are. And if we continue to look, we can see the logger who cut the tree and brought it to the mill to be transformed into paper. And we see wheat. We know that the logger cannot exist without his daily bread, and therefore the wheat that became his bread is also in this sheet of paper. The logger's father and mother are in it too. When we look in this way, we see that without all of these things, this sheet of paper cannot exist.

Looking even more deeply, we can see ourselves in this sheet of paper too. This is not difficult to see, because when we look at a sheet of paper, it is part of our perception. Your mind is in here and mine is also. So we can say that everything is in here with this sheet of paper. We cannot point out one thing that is not here—

time, space, the earth, the rain, the minerals in the soil, the sun-shine, the cloud, the river, the heat. Everything co-exists with this sheet of paper. That is why I think the word inter-be should be in the dictionary. "To be" is to inter-be. We cannot just *be* by our-selves alone. We have to inter-be with every other thing. This sheet of paper is, because everything else is.

Suppose we try to return one of the elements to its source. Suppose we return the sunshine to the sun. Do you think that this sheet of paper will be possible? No, without sunshine noth-ing can be. And if we return the logger to his mother, then we have no sheet of paper either. The fact is that this sheet of paper is made up only of "non-paper" elements. And if we return these non-paper elements to their sources, then there can be no paper at all. Without non-paper elements, like mind, logger, sunshine and so on, there will be no paper. As thin as this sheet of paper is, it contains everything in the universe in it.

Flowers and Garbage

Defiled or immaculate. Dirty or pure. These are concepts we form in our mind. A beautiful rose we have just cut and placed in our vase is pure. It smells so good, so fresh. A garbage can is the opposite. It smells horrible, and it is filled with rotten things.

But that is only when we look on the surface. If we look more deeply we will see that in just five or six days, the rose will become part of the garbage. We do not need to wait five days to see it. If we just look at the rose, and we look deeply, we can see it now. And if we look into the garbage can, we see that in a few months its contents can be transformed into lovely vegetables, and even a rose. If you are a good organic gardener, looking at a rose you can see the garbage, and looking at the garbage you can see a rose. Roses and garbage inter-are. Without a rose, we cannot have garbage; and without garbage, we cannot have a rose. They need each other very much. The rose and the garbage are equal. The garbage is just as precious as the rose. If we look deeply at the concepts of defilement and immaculateness, we return to the notion of interbeing.

In the city of Manila there are many young prostitutes; some are only fourteen or fifteen years old. They are very unhappy. They did not want to be prostitutes, but their families are poor and these young girls went to the city to look for some kind of job, like street vendor, to make money to send back to their families. Of course this is true not only in Manila, but in Ho Chi Minh City in Vietnam, in New York City, and in Paris also. After only a few weeks in the city, a vulnerable girl can be persuaded by a clever person to work for him and earn perhaps one hundred times more money than she could as a street vendor. Because she is so young and does not know much about life, she accepts and becomes a prostitute. Since that time, she has carried the feeling of being impure, defiled, and this causes her great suffering. When she looks at other young girls, dressed beautifully, belonging to good families, a wretched feeling wells up in her, a feeling of defilement that becomes her hell.

But if she could look deeply at herself and at the whole situation, she would see that she is the way she is because other people are the way they are. How can a "good girl," belonging to a good family, be proud? Because the "good family's" way of life is the way it is, the prostitute has to live as a prostitute. No one among us has clean hands. No one of us can claim that it is not our responsibility. The girl in Manila is that way because of the way we are. Looking into the life of that young prostitute, we see the lives of all the "non-prostitutes." And looking at the non-prostitutes and the way we live our lives, we see the prostitute. Each thing helps to create the other.

Let us look at wealth and poverty. The affluent society and the deprived society inter-are. The wealth of one society is made of the poverty of the other. "This is like this, because that is like that." Wealth is made of non-wealth elements, and poverty is made by non-poverty elements. It is exactly the same as with the sheet of paper. So we must be careful not to imprison ourselves in concepts. The truth is that everything contains everything else. We cannot just be, we can only inter-be. We are responsible for everything that happens around us.

Only by seeing with the eyes of interbeing can that young girl be freed from her suffering. Only then will she understand that she is bearing the burden of the whole world. What else can we offer her? Looking deeply into ourselves, we see her, and we will share her pain and the pain of the whole world. Then we can begin to be of real help.

Waging Peace

If the Earth were your body, you would be able to feel the many areas where it is suffering. War, political and economic oppression, famine, and pollution wreak havoc in so many places. Every day, children are becoming blind from malnutrition, their hands searching hopelessly through mounds of trash for a few ounces of food. Adults are dying slowly in prisons for trying to oppose violence. Rivers are dying, and the air is becoming more and more difficult to breathe. Although the two great superpowers are becoming a little more friendly, they still have enough nuclear weapons to destroy the Earth dozens of times.

Many people are aware of the world's suffering; their hearts are filled with compassion. They know what needs to be done, and they engage in political, social, and environmental work to try to change things. But after a period of intense involvement, they may become discouraged if they lack the strength needed to sustain a life of action. Real strength is not in power, money, or weapons, but in deep, inner peace.

Practicing mindfulness in each moment of our daily lives, we can cultivate our own peace. With clarity, determination, and patience—the fruits of meditation—we can sustain a life of action and be real instruments of peace. I have seen this peace in people of various religious and cultural backgrounds who spend their time and energy protecting the weak, struggling for social justice, lessening the disparity between rich and poor, stopping the arms race, fighting against discrimination, and watering the trees of love and understanding throughout the world.

Not Two

When we want to understand something, we cannot just stand outside and observe it. We have to enter deeply into it and be one with it in order to really understand. If we want to understand a person, we have to feel his feelings, suffer his sufferings, and enjoy his joy. The word "comprehend" is made up of the Latin roots *cum*, which means "with," and *prehendere*, which means "to grasp it or pick it up." To comprehend something means to pick it up and be one with it. There is no other way to understand something. In Buddhism, we call this kind of understanding "non-duality." Not two.

Fifteen years ago, I helped a committee for orphans who were victims of the war in Vietnam. From Vietnam, the social workers sent out applications, one sheet of paper with a small picture of a child in the corner, telling the name, age, and conditions of the orphan. My job was to translate the application from Vietnamese into French in order to seek a sponsor, so that the child would have food to eat and books for school, and be put into the family of an aunt, an uncle, or a grandparent. Then the committee in France could send the money to the family member to help take care of the child.

Each day I helped translate about thirty applications. The way I did it was to look at the picture of the child. I did not read the application, I just took time to look at the picture of the child. Usually after only thirty or forty seconds, I became one with the child. Then I would pick up the pen and translate the words from the application onto another sheet. Afterwards I realized that it was not me who had translated the application; it was the child and me, who had become one. Looking at his or her face, I felt inspired, and I became the child and he or she became me, and together we did the translation. It is very natural. You don't have to practice a lot of meditation to be able to do that. You just look, allowing yourself to be, and you lose yourself in the child, and the child in you.

Healing the Wounds of War

If only the United States had had the vision of non-duality concerning Vietnam, we would not have had so much destruction in both countries. The war continues to hurt both Americans and Vietnamese. If we are attentive enough, we can still learn from the war in Vietnam.

Last year we had a wonderful retreat with Vietnam veterans in America. It was a difficult retreat, because many of us could not get free of our pain. One gentleman told me that in Vietnam, he lost four hundred seventeen people in one battle alone, in one day. Four hundred seventeen men died in one battle, and he has had to live with that for more than fifteen years. Another person told me that out of anger and revenge, he took the life of children in a village, and after that, he lost all his peace. Ever since that time, he has not been able to sit alone with children in a room. There are many kinds of suffering, and they can prevent us from being in touch with the non-suffering world.

We must practice helping each other be in touch. One soldier told me that this retreat was the first time in fifteen years that he felt safe in a group of people. For fifteen years, he could not swallow solid food easily. He could only drink some fruit juice and eat some fruit. He was completely shut off and could not communicate. But after three or four days of practice, he began to open up and talk to people. You have to offer a lot of loving kindness in order to help such a person touch things again. During the retreat, we practiced mindful breathing and smiling, encouraging each other to come back to the flower in us, and to the trees and the blue sky that shelter us.

We had a silent breakfast. We practiced eating breakfast the way I ate the cookie of my childhood. We did things like that, making mindful steps in order to touch the Earth, breathing consciously in order to touch the air, and looking at our tea deeply in order to really be in touch with the tea. We sat together, breathed together, walked together, and tried to learn from our experience in Vietnam. The veterans have something to tell their nation about how to deal with other problems that are likely to happen, problems that will not look different from Vietnam. Out of our sufferings, we should learn something.

We need the vision of interbeing—we belong to each other; we cannot cut reality into pieces. The well-being of "this" is the well-being of "that," so we have to do things together. Every side is "our side"; there is no evil side. Veterans have experience that makes them the light at the tip of the candle, illuminating the roots of war and the way to peace.

The Sun My Heart

We know that if our heart stops beating, the flow of our life will stop, and so we cherish our heart very much. Yet we do not often take the time to notice that other things, outside of our bodies, are also essential for our survival. Look at the immense light we call the sun. If it were to stop shining, the flow of our life would also stop, so the sun is our second heart, a heart outside of our body. This immense "heart" gives all life on Earth the warmth necessary for existence. Plants live thanks to the sun. Their leaves absorb the sun's energy, along with carbon dioxide from the air, to produce food for the tree, the flower, the plankton. And thanks to plants, we and other animals can live. All of us—people, animals, and plants—consume the sun, directly and in-directly. We cannot begin to describe all the effects of the sun, that great heart outside of our body.

Our body is not limited to what is inside the boundary of our skin. It is much more immense. It includes even the layer of air around our Earth; for if the atmosphere were to disappear for even an instant, our life would end. There is no phenomenon in the universe that does not intimately concern us, from a pebble resting at the bottom of the ocean, to the movement of a galaxy millions of light-years away. Walt Whitman said, "I believe a leaf of grass is no less than the journey-work of the stars. . . ." These words are not philosophy. They come from the depths of his soul. He said, "I am large, I contain multitudes."

Looking Deeply

We have to look deeply at things in order to see. When a swimmer enjoys the clear water of the river, he or she should also be able to be the river. One day, during one of my first visits to the

United States, I was having lunch at Boston University with some friends, and I looked down at the Charles River. I had been away from home for quite a long time, and seeing the river, I found it very beautiful. So I left my friends and went down to wash my face and dip my feet in the water, as we used to do in our country. When I returned, a professor said, "That's a very dangerous thing to do. Did you rinse your mouth in the river?" When I told him yes, he said, "You should see a doctor and get a shot."

I was shocked. I hadn't known that the rivers here were so polluted. Some of them are called "dead rivers." In our country the rivers get very muddy sometimes, but not that kind of dirty. Someone told me that the Rhine River in Germany contains so many chemicals that it is possible to develop photographs in it. If we want to continue to enjoy our rivers—to swim in them, walk beside them, even drink their water—we have to adopt the non-dual perspective. We have to meditate on *being* the river so that we can experience within ourselves the fears and hopes of the river. If we cannot feel the rivers, the mountains, the air, the animals, and other people from within their own perspective, the rivers will die and we will lose our chance for peace.

If you are a mountain climber or someone who enjoys the countryside, or the green forest, you know that the forests are our lungs outside of our bodies, just as the sun is our heart outside of our bodies. Yet we have been acting in a way that has allowed two million square miles of forest land to be destroyed by acid rain, and we have destroyed parts of the ozone layer that regulate how much direct sunlight we receive. We are impris-

oned in our small selves, thinking only of the comfortable conditions for this small self, while we destroy our large self. We
should be able to be our true self. That means we should be able
to be the river, we should be able to be the forest, the sun, and the
ozone layer. We must do this to understand and to have hope for
the future.

The Art
of Mindful Living

Nature is our mother. Because we live cut off from her, we get
sick. Some of us live in boxes called apartments, very high above
the ground. Around us are only cement, metal, and hard things
like that. Our fingers do not have a chance to touch the soil; we
don't grow lettuce anymore. Because we are so distant from our
Mother Earth, we become sick. That is why we need to go out
from time to time and be in nature. It is very important. We and
our children should be in touch again with Mother Earth. In
many cities, we cannot see trees—the color green is entirely ab-
sent from our view.

One day, I imagined a city where there was only one tree left.
The tree was still beautiful, but very much alone, surrounded by

buildings, in the center of the city. Many people were getting sick, and most doctors did not know how to deal with the illness. But one very good doctor knew the causes of the sickness and gave this prescription to each patient: "Every day, take the bus and go to the center of the city to look at the tree. As you approach it, practice breathing in and out, and when you get there, hug the tree, breathing in and out for fifteen minutes, while you look at the tree, so green, and smell its bark, so fragrant. If you do that, in a few weeks you will feel much better."

The people began to feel better, but very soon there were so many people rushing to the tree that they stood in line for miles and miles. You know that people of our time do not have much patience, so standing three or four hours to wait to hug the tree was too much, and they rebelled. They organized demonstrations in order to make a new law that each person could only hug the tree for five minutes, but of course that reduced the time for healing. And soon, the time was reduced to one minute, and the chance of being healed by our mother was lost.

We could be in that situation very soon if we are not mindful. We have to practice awareness of each thing we do if we want to save our Mother Earth, and ourselves and our children as well. For example, when we look into our garbage, we can see lettuce, cucumbers, tomatoes, and flowers. When we throw a banana peel into the garbage, we are aware that it is a banana peel that we are throwing out and that it will be transformed into a flower or a vegetable very soon. That is exactly the practice of meditation.

When we throw a plastic bag into the garbage, we know that

it is different from a banana peel. It will take a long time to become a flower. "Throwing a plastic bag into the garbage, I know that I am throwing a plastic bag into the garbage." That awareness alone helps us protect the Earth, make peace, and take care of life in the present moment and in the future. If we are aware, naturally we will try to use fewer plastic bags. This is an act of peace, a basic kind of peace action.

When we throw a plastic disposable diaper into the garbage, we know that it takes even longer for it to become a flower, four hundred years or longer. Knowing that using these kinds of diapers is not in the direction of peace, we look for other ways to take care of our baby. Practicing breathing and contemplating our body, feelings, mind, and objects of mind, we practice peace in the present moment. This is living mindfully.

Nuclear waste is the worst kind of garbage. It takes about 250,000 years to become flowers. Forty of the fifty United States are already polluted by nuclear waste. We are making the Earth an impossible place to live for ourselves and for many generations of children. If we live our present moment mindfully, we will know what to do and what not to do, and we will try to do things in the direction of peace.

Nourishing Awareness

When we sit down to dinner and look at our plate filled with fragrant and appetizing food, we can nourish our awareness of the bitter pain of people who suffer from hunger. Every day, 40,000 children die as a result of hunger and malnutrition. Every day! Such a figure shocks us every time we hear it. Looking deeply at our plate, we can "see" Mother Earth, the farm workers, and the tragedy of hunger and malnutrition.

We who live in North America and Europe are accustomed to eating grains and other foods imported from the Third World, such as coffee from Colombia, chocolate from Ghana, or fragrant rice from Thailand. We must be aware that children in these countries, except those from rich families, never see such fine products. They eat inferior foods, while the finer products are put aside for export in order to bring in foreign exchange. There are even some parents who, because they do not have the means to feed their children, resort to selling their children to be servants to families who have enough to eat.

Before each meal, we can join our palms in mindfulness and think about the children who do not have enough to eat. Doing so will help us maintain mindfulness of our good fortune, and perhaps one day we will find ways to do something to help change the system of injustice that exists in the world. In many refugee families, before each meal, a child holds up his bowl of rice and says something like this: "Today, on the table, there are many delicious foods. I am grateful to be here with my family enjoying these wonderful dishes. I know there are many children less fortunate, who are very hungry." Being a refugee he knows, for example, that most Thai children never see the kind of fine rice grown in Thailand that he is about to eat. It is difficult to explain to children in the "overdeveloped" nations that not all children in the world have such beautiful and nourishing food. Awareness of this fact alone can help us overcome many of our own psychological pains. Eventually our contemplations can help us see how to assist those who need our help so much.

A Love Letter
to Your Congressman

In the peace movement there is a lot of anger, frustration, and misunderstanding. People in the peace movement can write very good protest letters, but they are not so skilled at writing love letters. We need to learn to write letters to the Congress and the President that they will want to read, and not just throw away. The way we speak, the kind of understanding, the kind of language we use should not turn people off. The President is a person like any of us.

Can the peace movement talk in loving speech, showing the way for peace? I think that will depend on whether the people in the peace movement can "be peace." Because without being peace, we cannot do anything for peace. If we cannot smile, we cannot help other people smile. If we are not peaceful, then we cannot contribute to the peace movement.

I hope we can offer a new dimension to the peace movement. The peace movement often is filled with anger and hatred and does not fulfill the role we expect of it. A fresh way of being peace, of making peace is needed. That is why it is so important for us to practice mindfulness, to acquire the capacity to look, to see, and to understand. It would be wonderful if we could bring to the peace movement our non-dualistic way of looking at things. That alone would diminish hatred and aggression. Peace work means, first of all, being peace. We rely on each other. Our children are relying on us in order for them to have a future.

Citizenship

As citizens, we have a large responsibility. Our daily lives, the way we drink, what we eat, have to do with the world's political situation. Every day we do things, we are things, that have to do with peace. If we are aware of our lifestyle, our way of consuming, of looking at things, we will know how to make peace right in the moment we are alive. We think that our government is free to make any policy it wishes, but that freedom depends on our daily life. If we make it possible for them to change policies, they will do it. Now it is not yet possible.

You may think that if you were to enter government and obtain power, you would be able to do anything you wanted, but that is not true. If you became President, you would be confronted by this hard fact—you would probably do almost exactly the same thing as our current President, perhaps a little better, perhaps a little worse.

Meditation is to look deeply into things and to see how we can change ourselves and how we can transform our situation. To transform our situation is also to transform our minds. To transform our minds is also to transform our situation, because the situation is mind, and mind is situation. Awakening is important. The nature of the bombs, the nature of injustice, and the nature of our own beings are the same.

As we ourselves begin to live more responsibly, we must ask our political leaders to move in the same direction. We have to encourage them to stop polluting our environment and our consciousness. We should help them appoint advisors who share our way of thinking about peace, so that they can turn to these people for advice and support. It will require some degree of enlightenment on our part to support our political leaders, especially when they are campaigning for office. We have the opportunity to tell them about many important things, instead of choosing leaders by how handsome they look on television and then feeling discouraged later by their lack of mindfulness.

If we write articles and give speeches that express our conviction that political leaders should be helped by those who practice mindfulness, those who have a deep sense of calm and peace and a clear vision of what the world should be, we will begin to elect leaders who can help us move in the direction of peace. The French government has made some efforts in this direction, appointing as Ministers a number of ecologists and humanitarians, such as Bernard Cushman, who helped rescue boat people on the Gulf of Siam. This kind of attitude is a good sign.

Ecology of Mind

We need harmony, we need peace. Peace is based on respect for life, the spirit of reverence for life. Not only do we have to respect the lives of human beings, but we have to respect the lives of animals, vegetables, and minerals. Rocks can be alive. A rock can be destroyed. The Earth also. The destruction of our health by pollution of the air and water is linked to the destruction of the minerals. The way we farm, the way we deal with our garbage, all these things are related to each other.

Ecology should be a deep ecology. Not only deep but universal, because there is pollution in our consciousness. Television, for instance, is a form of pollution for us and for our children. Television sows seeds of violence and anxiety in our children, and pollutes their consciousness, just as we destroy our environment by chemicals, tree-cutting, and polluting the water. We need to protect the ecology of the mind, or this kind of violence and recklessness will continue to spill over into many other areas of life.

The Roots of War

In 1966, when I was in the U.S. calling for a ceasefire to the war in Vietnam, a young American peace activist stood up during a talk I was giving and shouted, "The best thing you can do is go back to your country and defeat the American aggressors! You shouldn't be here. There is absolutely no use to your being here!"

He and many Americans wanted peace, but the kind of peace they wanted was the defeat of one side in order to satisfy their anger. Because they had called for a ceasefire and had not succeeded, they became angry, and finally they were unable to accept any solution short of the defeat of their own country. But we Vietnamese who were suffering under the bombs had to be more realistic. We wanted peace. We did not care about anyone's victory or defeat. We just wanted the bombs to stop falling on us. But many people in the peace movement opposed our proposal for an immediate ceasefire. No one seemed to understand.

So when I heard that young man shouting, "Go home and defeat the American aggressors," I took several deep breaths to regain myself, and I said, "Sir, it seems to me that many of the roots of the war are here in your country. That is why I have come. One of the roots is your way of seeing the world. Both sides are victims of a wrong policy, a policy that believes in the force of violence to settle problems. I do not want Vietnamese to die, and I do not want American soldiers to die either."

The roots of war are in the way we live our daily lives—the way we develop our industries, build up our society, and consume goods. We have to look deeply into the situation, and we will see the roots of war. We cannot just blame one side or the other. We have to transcend the tendency to take sides.

During any conflict, we need people who can understand the suffering of all sides. For example, if a number of people in South Africa could go to each side and understand their suffering, and communicate that to the other sides, that would be very helpful. We need links. We need communication.

Practicing nonviolence is first of all to become nonviolence. Then when a difficult situation presents itself, we will react in a way that will help the situation. This applies to problems of the family as well as to problems of society.

Like a Leaf,
We Have Many Stems

One autumn day, I was in a park, absorbed in the contemplation of a very small, beautiful leaf, shaped like a heart. Its color was almost red, and it was barely hanging on the branch, nearly ready to fall down. I spent a long time with it, and I asked the leaf a number of questions. I found out the leaf had been a mother to the tree. Usually we think that the tree is the mother and the leaves are just children, but as I looked at the leaf I saw that the leaf is also a mother to the tree. The sap that the roots take up is only water and minerals, not sufficient to nourish the tree. So the tree distributes that sap to the leaves, and the leaves transform the rough sap into elaborated sap and, with the help of the sun and gas, send it back to the tree for nourishment. Therefore, the leaves are also the mother to the tree. Since the leaf is linked to the tree by a stem, the communication between them is easy to see.

We do not have a stem linking us to our mother anymore, but when we were in her womb, we had a very long stem, an umbilical cord. The oxygen and the nourishment we needed came to us through that stem. But on the day we were born, it was cut off, and we received the illusion that we became independent. That is not true. We continue to rely on our mother for a very long time, and we have many other mothers as well. The Earth is our mother. We have a great many stems linking us to our Mother Earth. There are stems linking us with the clouds. If there are no clouds, there will be no water for us to drink. We are made of at least seventy percent water, and the stem between the cloud and us is really there. This is also the case with the river, the forest, the logger, and the farmer. There are hundreds of thousands of stems linking us to everything in the cosmos, supporting us and making it possible for us to be. Do you see the link between you and me? If you are not there, I am not here. This is certain. If you do not see it yet, please look more deeply and I am sure you will.

I asked the leaf whether it was frightened because it was autumn and the other leaves were falling. The leaf told me, "No. During the whole spring and summer I was completely alive. I worked hard to help nourish the tree, and now much of me is in the tree. I am not limited by this form. I am also the whole tree, and when I go back to the soil, I will continue to nourish the tree. So I don't worry at all. As I leave this branch and float to the ground, I will wave to the tree and tell her, 'I will see you again very soon.'"

That day there was a wind blowing and, after a while, I saw the leaf leave the branch and float down to the soil, dancing joyfully, because as it floated it saw itself already there in the tree. It was so happy. I bowed my head, knowing that I have a lot to learn from that leaf.

We Are All
Linked to Each Other

Millions of people follow sports. If you love to watch soccer or baseball, you probably root for one team and identify with them. You may watch the games with despair and elation. Perhaps you give a little kick or swing to help the ball along. If you do not take sides, the fun is missing. In wars we also pick sides, usually the side that is being threatened. Peace movements are born of this feeling. We get angry, we shout, but rarely do we rise above all this to look at a conflict the way a mother would who is watching her two children fighting. She seeks only their reconciliation.

"In order to fight each other, the chicks born from the same mother hen put colors on their faces." This is a well-known Vietnamese saying. Putting colors on our own face is to make ourselves a stranger to our own brothers and sisters. We can only shoot others when they are strangers. Real efforts for reconciliation arise when we see with the eyes of compassion, and that ability comes when we see clearly the nature of interbeing and interpenetration of all beings.

In our lives, we may be lucky enough to know someone whose love extends to animals and plants. We may also know people who, although they themselves live in a safe situation, realize that famine, disease, and oppression are destroying millions of people on Earth and look for ways to help those who suffer. They cannot forget the downtrodden, even amidst the pressures of their own lives. At least to some extent, these people have realized the interdependent nature of life. They know that the survival of the underdeveloped countries cannot be separated from the survival of the materially wealthy, technically advanced countries. Poverty and oppression bring war. In our times, every war involves all countries. The fate of each country is linked to the fate of all others.

When will the chicks of the same mother hen remove the colors from their faces and recognize each other as brothers and sisters? The only way to end the danger is for each of us to do so, and to say to others, "I am your brother." "I am your sister." "We are all humankind, and our life is one."

Reconciliation

What can we do when we have hurt people and now they consider us to be their enemy? These people might be people in our family, in our community, or in another country. I think you know the answer. There are few things to do. The first thing is to take the time to say, "I am sorry, I hurt you out of my ignorance, out of my lack of mindfulness, out of my lack of skillfulness. I will try my best to change myself. I don't dare to say anything more to you." Sometimes, we do not have the intention to hurt, but because we are not mindful or skillful enough, we hurt someone. Being mindful in our daily life is important, speaking in a way that will not hurt anyone.

The second thing to do is to try to bring out the best part in ourselves, the part of the flower, to transform ourselves. That is the only way to demonstrate what you have just said. When you have become fresh and pleasant, the other person will notice very soon. Then when there is a chance to approach that person, you can come to her as a flower and she will notice immediately that you are quite different. You may not have to say anything. Just seeing you like that, she will accept you and forgive you. That is called "speaking with your life and not just with words."

When you begin to see that your enemy is suffering, that is the beginning of insight. When you see in yourself the wish that the other person stop suffering, that is a sign of real love. But be careful. Sometimes you may think that you are stronger than you actually are. To test your real strength, try going to the other person to listen and talk to him or her, and you will discover right away whether your loving compassion is real. You need the other person in order to test. If you just meditate on some abstract principle such as understanding or love, it may be just your imagination and not real understanding or real love.

Reconciliation does not mean to sign an agreement with duplicity and cruelty. Reconciliation opposes all forms of ambition, without taking sides. Most of us want to take sides in each encounter or conflict. We distinguish right from wrong based on partial evidence or hearsay. We need indignation in order to act, but even righteous, legitimate indignation is not enough. Our world does not lack people willing to throw themselves into action. What we need are people who are capable of loving, of not taking sides so that they can embrace the whole of reality.

We have to continue to practice mindfulness and reconciliation until we can see a child's body of skin and bones in Uganda or Ethiopia as our own, until the hunger and pain in the bodies of all species are our own. Then we will have realized non-discrimination, real love. Then we can look at all beings with the eyes of compassion, and we can do the real work to help alleviate suffering.

Call Me by
My True Names

In Plum Village, where I live in France, we receive many letters from the refugee camps in Singapore, Malaysia, Indonesia, Thailand, and the Philippines, hundreds each week. It is very painful to read them, but we have to do it, we have to be in contact. We try our best to help, but the suffering is enormous, and sometimes we are discouraged. It is said that half the boat people die in the ocean. Only half arrive at the shores in Southeast Asia, and even then they may not be safe.

There are many young girls, boat people, who are raped by sea pirates. Even though the United Nations and many countries try to help the government of Thailand prevent that kind of piracy, sea pirates continue to inflict much suffering on the refugees. One day we received a letter telling us about a young girl on a small boat who was raped by a Thai pirate. She was only twelve, and she jumped into the ocean and drowned herself.

When you first learn of something like that, you get angry at the pirate. You naturally take the side of the girl. As you look more deeply you will see it differently. If you take the side of the little girl, then it is easy. You only have to take a gun and shoot the pirate. But we cannot do that. In my meditation I saw that if I had been born in the village of the pirate and raised in the same conditions as he was, there is a great likelihood that I would become a pirate. I saw that many babies are born along the Gulf of Siam, hundreds every day, and if we educators, social workers, politicians, and others do not do something about the situation, in twenty-five years a number of them will become sea pirates. That is certain. If you or I were born today in those fishing villages, we may become sea pirates in twenty-five years. If you take a gun and shoot the pirate, you shoot all of us, because all of us are to some extent responsible for this state of affairs.

After a long meditation, I wrote this poem. In it, there are three people: the twelve-year-old girl, the pirate, and me. Can we look at each other and recognize ourselves in each other? The

title of the poem is "Please Call Me by My True Names," because
I have so many names. When I hear one of these names, I have
to say, "Yes."

Do not say that I'll depart tomorrow
because even today I still arrive.

Look deeply: I arrive in every second
to be a bud on a spring branch,
to be a tiny bird, with wings still fragile,
learning to sing in my new nest,
to be a caterpillar in the heart of a flower,
to be a jewel hiding itself in a stone.

I still arrive, in order to laugh and to cry,
in order to fear and to hope.
The rhythm of my heart is the birth and
death of all that are alive.

I am the mayfly metamorphosing on the surface of the river,
and I am the bird which, when spring comes, arrives in time
            to eat the mayfly.

I am the frog swimming happily in the clear pond,
and I am also the grass-snake who, approaching in silence,
            feeds itself on the frog.

I am the child in Uganda, all skin and bones,
my legs as thin as bamboo sticks,
and I am the arms merchant, selling deadly weapons to
            Uganda.

I am the twelve-year-old girl, refugee on a small boat,
who throws herself into the ocean after being raped by a sea
*   pirate,*
and I am the pirate, my heart not yet capable of seeing and
*   loving.*

I am a member of the politburo, with plenty of power in my
*   hands,*
and I am the man who has to pay his "debt of blood" to my
*   people,*
dying slowly in a forced labor camp.

My joy is like spring, so warm it makes flowers bloom in all
*   walks of life.*
My pain is like a river of tears, so full it fills the four oceans.

Please call me by my true names,
so I can hear all my cries and laughs at once,
so I can see that my joy and pain are one.

Please call me by my true names,
so I can wake up,
and so the door of my heart can be left open,
the door of compassion.

Suffering
Nourishes Compassion

We have been practicing "engaged Buddhism" in Vietnam for the last thirty years. During the war, we could not just sit in the meditation hall. We had to practice mindfulness everywhere, especially where the worst suffering was going on.

Being in touch with the kind of suffering we encountered during the war can heal us of some of the suffering we experience when our lives are not very meaningful or useful. When you confront the kinds of difficulties we faced during the war, you see that you can be a source of compassion and a great help to many suffering people. In that intense suffering, you feel a kind of relief and joy within yourself, because you know that you are an instrument of compassion. Understanding such intense suffering and realizing compassion in the midst of it, you become a joyful person, even if your life is very hard.

Last winter, some friends and I went to visit the refugee camps in Hong Kong, and we witnessed a lot of suffering. There were "boat people" who were just one or two years old, who were about to be sent back to their country because they were classified as illegal immigrants. They had lost both father and mother during the trip. When you see that kind of suffering, you know that the suffering your friends in Europe and America are undergoing is not very great.

Every time we come back from such a contact, we see that the city of Paris is not very real. The way people live there and the reality of the suffering in other parts of the world are so different. I asked the question, how could people live like this when things are like that? But if you stay in Paris for ten years without being in touch, you find it normal.

Meditation is a point of contact. Sometimes you do not have to go to the place of suffering. You just sit quietly on your cushion, and you can see everything. You can actualize everything, and you can be aware of what is going on in the world. Out of that kind of awareness, compassion and understanding arise naturally, and you can stay right in your own country and perform social action.

Love in Action

During our journey together, I have presented a number of practices to help us maintain mindfulness of what is going on inside us and immediately around us. Now, as we make our way through the wider world, some additional guidelines can help us and protect us. Several members of our community have been practicing the following principles, and I think you may also find them useful in making choices as to how to live in our contemporary world. We call them the fourteen precepts of the Order of Interbeing.

1. Do not be idolatrous about or bound to any doctrine, theory, or ideology. All systems of thought are guiding means; they are not absolute truth.

2. Do not think that the knowledge you presently possess is changeless, absolute truth. Avoid being narrow-minded and bound to present views. Learn and practice non-attachment from views in order to be open to receive others' viewpoints. Truth is found in life and not merely in conceptual knowledge. Be ready to learn throughout your entire life and to observe reality in yourself and in the world at all times.

3. Do not force others, including children, by any means whatsoever, to adopt your views, whether by authority, threat, money, propaganda, or even education. However, through compassionate dialogue, help others renounce fanaticism and narrowness.

4. Do not avoid contact with suffering or close your eyes before suffering. Do not lose awareness of the existence of suffering

in the life of the world. Find ways to be with those who are suffering, by all means, including personal contact and visits, images, and sound. By such means, awaken yourself and others to the reality of suffering in the world.

5. Do not accumulate wealth while millions are hungry. Do not take as the aim of your life fame, profit, wealth, or sensual pleasure. Live simply and share time, energy, and material resources with those who are in need.

6. Do not maintain anger or hatred. Learn to penetrate and transform them while they are still seeds in your consciousness. As soon as anger or hatred arises, turn your attention to your breathing in order to see and understand the nature of your anger or hatred and the nature of the persons who have caused your anger or hatred.

7. Do not lose yourself in dispersion and in your surroundings. Practice mindful breathing in order to come back to what is happening in the present moment. Be in touch with what is wondrous, refreshing, and healing, both inside and around yourself. Plant the seeds of joy, peace, and understanding in yourself in order to facilitate the work of transformation in the depths of your consciousness.

8. Do not utter words that can create discord and cause the community to break. Make every effort to reconcile and resolve all conflicts, however small.

9. Do not say untruthful things for the sake of personal interest or to impress people. Do not utter words that cause division and hatred. Do not spread news that you do not know to be certain. Do not criticize or condemn things that you are not sure of. Always speak truthfully and constructively. Have the courage to speak out about situations of injustice, even when doing so may threaten your own safety.

10. Do not use the religious community for personal gain or profit, or transform your community into a political party. A religious community should, however, take a clear stand against oppression and injustice, and should strive to change the situation without engaging in partisan conflicts.

11. Do not live with a vocation that is harmful to humans and nature. Do not invest in companies that deprive others of their chance to live. Select a vocation that helps realize your ideal of compassion.

12. Do not kill. Do not let others kill. Find whatever means possible to protect life and prevent war.

13. Possess nothing that should belong to others. Respect the property of others but prevent others from enriching themselves from human suffering or the suffering of other beings.

14. Do not mistreat your body. Learn to handle it with respect. Do not look on your body as only an instrument. Preserve

vital energies for the realization of the Way. Sexual expression should not happen without love and commitment. In sexual relationships, be aware of future suffering that may be caused. To preserve the happiness of others, respect the rights and commitments of others. Be fully aware of the responsibility of bringing new lives into the world. Meditate on the world into which you are bringing new beings.

The River

Once upon a time there was a beautiful river finding her way among the hills, forests, and meadows. She began by being a joyful stream of water, a spring always dancing and singing as she ran down from the top of the mountain. She was very young at the time, and as she came to the lowland she slowed down. She was thinking about going to the ocean. As she grew up, she learned to look beautiful, winding gracefully among the hills and meadows.

One day she noticed the clouds within herself. Clouds of all sorts of colors and forms. She did nothing during these days but chase after clouds. She wanted to possess a cloud, to have one for herself. But clouds float and travel in the sky, and they are always changing their form. Sometimes they look like an overcoat, sometimes like a horse. Because of the nature of impermanence within the clouds, the river suffered very much. Her pleasure, her joy had become just chasing after clouds, one after another, but despair, anger, and hatred became her life.

Then one day a strong wind came and blew away all the clouds in the sky. The sky became completely empty. Our river thought that life was not worth living, for there were no longer any clouds to chase after. She wanted to die. "If there are no clouds, why should I be alive?" But how can a river take her own life?

That night the river had the opportunity to go back to herself for the first time. She had been running for so long after something outside of herself that she had never seen herself. That night was the first opportunity for her to hear her own crying, the sounds of water crashing against the banks of the river. Because she was able to listen to her own voice, she discovered something quite important.

She realized that what she had been looking for was already in herself. She found out that clouds are nothing but water. Clouds are born from water and will return to water. And she found out that she herself is also water.

The next morning when the sun was in the sky, she discovered something beautiful. She saw the blue sky for the first time. She had never noticed it before. She had only been interested in clouds, and she had missed seeing the sky, which is the home of all the clouds. Clouds are impermanent, but the sky is stable. She realized that the immense sky had been within her heart since the very beginning. This great insight brought her peace and happiness. As she saw the vast wonderful blue sky, she knew that her peace and stability would never be lost again.

That afternoon the clouds returned, but this time she did not want to possess any of them. She could see the beauty of each cloud, and she was able to welcome all of them. When a cloud came by, she would greet him or her with loving kindness. When that cloud wanted to go away, she would wave to him or her happily and with loving kindness. She realized that all clouds are her. She didn't have to choose between the clouds and herself. Peace and harmony existed between her and the clouds.

That evening something wonderful happened. When she opened her heart completely to the evening sky she received the image of the full moon—beautiful, round, like a jewel within herself. She had never imagined that she could receive such a beautiful image. There is a very beautiful poem in Chinese: "The fresh and beautiful moon is travelling in the utmost empty sky. When the mind-rivers of living beings are free, that image of the beautiful moon will reflect in each of us."

This was the mind of the river at that moment. She received the image of that beautiful moon within her heart, and water, clouds, and moon took each other's hands and practiced walking meditation slowly, slowly to the ocean.

There is nothing to chase after. We can go back to ourselves, enjoy our breathing, our smiling, ourselves, and our beautiful environment.

Entering the
Twenty-First Century

·The word "policy" is very much in use these days. There seems to be a policy for just about everything. I have heard that the so-called developed nations are contemplating a garbage policy to send their trash on huge barges to the Third World.

I think that we need a "policy" for dealing with our suffering. We do not want to condone it, but we need to find a way to make use of our suffering, for our good and for the good of others. There has been so much suffering in the twentieth century: two world wars, concentration camps in Europe, the killing fields of Cambodia, refugees from Vietnam, Central America, and elsewhere fleeing their countries with no place to land. We need to articulate a policy for these kinds of garbage also. We need to use the suffering of the twentieth century as compost, so that together we can create flowers for the twenty-first century.

When we see photographs and programs about the atrocities of the Nazis, the gas chambers and the camps, we feel afraid. We may say, "I didn't do it; they did it." But if we had been there, we may have done the same thing, or we may have been too cowardly to stop it, as was the case for so many. We have to put all these things into our compost pile to fertilize the ground. In Germany today, the young people have a kind of complex that they are somehow responsible for the suffering. It is important that these young people and the generation responsible for the war begin anew, and together create a path of mindfulness so that our children in the next century can avoid repeating the same mistakes. The flower of tolerance to see and appreciate cultural diversity is one flower we can cultivate for the children of the twenty-first century. Another flower is the truth of suffering—there has been so much unnecessary suffering in our century. If we are willing to work together and learn together, we can all benefit from the mistakes of our time, and, seeing with the eyes of compassion and understanding, we can offer the next century a beautiful garden and a clear path.

Take the hand of your child and invite her to go out and sit with you on the grass. The two of you may want to contemplate the green grass, the little flowers that grow among the grasses, and the sky. Breathing and smiling together—that is peace education. If we know how to appreciate these beautiful things, we will not have to search for anything else. Peace is available in every moment, in every breath, in every step.

I have enjoyed our journey together. I hope you have enjoyed it too. We shall see each other again.

About the Author

Thich Nhat Hanh was born in central Vietnam in 1926, and he left home as a teenager to become a Zen monk. In Vietnam, he founded the School of Youth for Social Service, Van Hanh Buddhist University, and the Tiep Hien Order (Order of Interbeing). He has taught at Columbia University and the Sorbonne, was Chair of the Vietnamese Buddhist Peace Delegation to the Paris Peace Talks, and was nominated by Martin Luther King, Jr. for the Nobel Peace Prize. Since 1966, he has lived in exile in France, where he continues his writing, teaching, gardening, and helping refugees worldwide. He is the author of seventy-five books in English, French, and Vietnamese, including *Being Peace*, *The Miracle of Mindfulness*, and *The Sun My Heart*.

About the Editor

Arnold Kotler was an ordained student at the San Francisco and Tassajara Zen Centers from 1969 to 1984. He is the founding editor of Parallax Press, a publishing company in Berkeley, California, dedicated to producing books and tapes on mindful awareness and social responsibility, including the works of Thich Nhat Hanh.

For a catalogue of books and tapes by Thich Nhat Hanh, or a current schedule of Thich Nhat Hanh's lectures and retreats worldwide, please contact:

Parallax Press
P.O. Box 7355
Berkeley, California 94707